HOW TO STOP SMOKING
AND STAY STOPPED FOR GOOD

D0543634

HOW TO STOP SMOKING AND STAY STOPPED FOR GOOD

Gillian Riley

VERMILION
LONDON

Published in Great Britain by Vermilion
an imprint of the Random Century Group
Random Century House
20 Vauxhall Bridge Road
London SW1V 2SA

British Library Cataloguing-in-Publication Data
Riley, Gillian
   How to stop smoking and stay stopped for good.
   I. Title
   362.29

   ISBN 0-09-175178-0

Typeset in Trump Medieval by Tek Art Ltd, Addiscombe, Croydon, Surrey

Printed and bound in Great Britain by Mackays of Chatham Plc, Kent

CONTENTS

*F*OREWORD

How To Stop Smoking And Stay Stopped For Good is profoundly different from any other book or technique I have come across in this area. It is an innovative application of traditional cognitive psychology and it has had a rate of success unique in the field of smoking cessation.

Gillian Riley offers the insights she has gained through ten years of intensive counselling with smokers. And she has worked with them, not only while they are in the initial process of stopping smoking, but also for many months afterwards. She supports her approach with personal case histories and research material, and presents challenging and complex information in a way that is entirely accessible to a popular audience.

I would strongly encourage researchers in the field of addiction to study these techniques. I believe that they shed new and original light on the addiction to smoking and, most intriguingly, they apply to the treatment of other addictions as well.

This cost-effective approach deserves to reach the widest possible public. It would help millions of smokers to stop smoking. And diminished rates of respiratory, heart and malignant diseases would result in substantial material savings for individuals, corporations, and overburdened health care systems.

Dr Roy Eskapa, AFBPsS
Clinical Psychologist

PREFACE

Anyone who has ever wanted to stop smoking has dreamed of a magic cure — an easy, effortless solution that takes the whole problem away. Smokers often want to find a way to stop and never doubt their decision, never feel tempted to smoke again and therefore never fear failure.

Most therapies and techniques encourage this dream. Those people who threaten, needle, shock and hypnotise smokers into stopping focus on a process that reinforces the decision to quit, promising permanent success if this first step is taken.

But it is one thing to stop smoking and quite another thing to stay stopped. In one article, a hypnotist claims a ninety per cent success rate. Another, in his book, claims that eighty per cent succeed with his method. But neither give any reference to how long these ex-smokers remained 'cured' — five minutes? Five weeks? Without that information, these claims are virtually meaningless.

According to the Addiction Research Unit at the University of London, eighty per cent of smokers who have given up return to smoking within a year.

Perhaps you could say that if these people go back to smoking later on, it's their own fault. But could it be that there are crucial flaws in the techniques employed; flaws that will inevitably lead the great majority of ex-smokers back to their old ways?

How To Stop Smoking And Stay Stopped For Good regards stopping smoking not as an event, but as part of a process. The process begins even before stopping and continues long after the last cigarette has been extinguished.

This is because stopping smoking is really about changing the way you think as a smoker. It is a matter of becoming aware of the addiction in the mind and resolving the conflicts it creates. And that doesn't happen in an instant, like magic.

For you, this is both good news and bad news. The bad news is that it's not just a matter of deciding to stop and toughing it out for a few days. Most smokers have already done that at some time and still gone back to smoking after weeks or months of abstinence.

The good news is that if you recognise and understand the mental aspect of the addiction, you have a far greater chance of long-term success than if you try to pretend that it isn't there.

Every smoker is different, but they all have much in common: a powerful, insidious and often underestimated drug addiction. If you cannot grasp how this addiction works, no amount of motivation or willpower will enable you to succeed in the long-term.

Stopping smoking is the first giant step, but it's not just a matter of stopping. It's learning the skill of staying stopped that's the real challenge. And that's what this book is all about.

PART ONE
UNDERSTANDING ADDICTION

---

1 | *HOW TO USE THIS BOOK*

'Our remedies oft in ourselves do lie
Which we ascribe to heaven.'

William Shakespeare, *All's Well That Ends Well*

THE technique that this book describes is radically
different from any other you will have come across.
Although the message may at times seem obvious, in
practice it requires a change in your mental approach which
needs to be worked at. It will challenge the way you have
been thinking about smoking and will require you to
question and absorb completely new ideas. This takes time,
and the most valuable thing you can do is to make stopping
smoking the number one priority in your life while you are
going through this major change.

The way to learn this technique is to read this book
thoroughly, frequently and, most important of all, privately.
As far as possible, tell no-one that you are thinking about
stopping smoking, don't discuss what you are doing in the
process of stopping, and try to keep quiet for as long as you
can about having stopped, when you do. This may seem
unusual, but there are some very good reasons for doing it
this way.

It's not that your smoking doesn't affect other people, because it does. And it's not that other people aren't entitled to their opinion about your smoking, because they are. The reason that it's best to keep it to yourself is because the first step for you in taking control of your smoking is to recognise that your smoking is a problem *you* have created, and it's *your* problem to solve.

If you keep this technique private, you will learn to rely completely on yourself, and therefore you will be able to stay stopped, no matter who is or isn't with you. It can make the difference between success and failure if you can remember that whether you smoke or not is entirely up to you. It will also help you to stop smoking — and stay stopped — because *you* want to, and not to please others.

If friends or family know you are reading this book, tell them you don't want to discuss it. The whole process of stopping smoking will be, and needs to be, on your mind a lot to begin with, so it can be very tempting to keep talking about it. But if you do, you will invite their comments, and encouragement and advice from other people can so easily end up feeling like pressure or nagging.

I think that you will understand more clearly the value of keeping this private as you read on, but it's important to put this into practice from the beginning.

If you and your partner both want to stop, my advice is not to stop smoking at the same time. You can get competitive, resentful of each other's failure or success, and your own motivation can get tied up with wanting the other to succeed. If you do stop smoking at the same time as a partner or friend, at least don't discuss it at all during the first few weeks.

You might believe it's impossible for you to stop smoking unless your partner or friend stops as well. But you will find, as many others have, that one of the best things about this technique is that you will have no difficulty spending time with other smokers after you have stopped.

You might, however, want to create or join a support group, or have one person, a counsellor for example, to talk things through with. This won't counteract the benefit of keeping the process private if you make sure you discuss stopping smoking *only* with that group or person, and *only* at specific times. This is entirely different from talking about stopping at home, during work or on social occasions with anyone who will listen.

If you do use a group or support person, make sure they don't have a vested interest in you stopping smoking. In other words, if someone in your life has been pushing you to stop smoking, they are *not* the person to ask for support.

And it's going to be very important for the person or people who are supporting you to be familiar with this technique. Otherwise, they will inevitably advise you in ways that are contrary to this approach.

How much time you spend reading and at what point you stop smoking is entirely up to you. You might read this book through once and become inspired to stop immediately. Or it may be that it won't start to make any real sense until you have read it through a number of times.

This has very little to do with how intelligent you are and a great deal to do with how addicted you are. Because the central ideas require a complete revision of your habitual way of thinking, it might take a while for you to get used to and really understand them.

If you think that a particular chapter has just clicked something vital into place in your mind, whether it's on your first reading or your twentieth, by all means go ahead and stop smoking there and then. If you decide to stop during your first read, make sure that you are able to finish the whole book as soon as possible, because there will almost certainly be some crucial information for you in each chapter.

If, however, you get to the end and still don't feel ready to stop, then I suggest that you read and re-read, and then set a target date for stopping. Write it down, with a specific time, so that you don't conveniently 'forget' it; and keep working with the technique to overcome your resistance to making this change.

This book will act as your support system, so it's very important that you continue to read it once you have stopped, and keep coming back to review what you have read for weeks and even months after.

Hang on to your own copy of this book, underline things and write comments for yourself: the more you get involved with it, the more real it will become to you and the more likely you are to succeed.

In Part One I will explain *why* this technique works; Part Two will show you *how* to put it into practice. The index will help you locate specific information you may want to return to. In between the chapters are contributions from people who have attended my course, describing in their own words how this technique worked for them.

Throughout the book I have referred exclusively to the activity of smoking cigarettes. This is out of brevity and because the vast majority of those addicted to nicotine take their drug in this form. Exactly the same technique applies, however, to anyone wanting to take control of nicotine addiction in any form, including cigars, pipes, snuff, chewing tobacco, and nicotine gum.

I strongly advise you against using other stop-smoking techniques together with this one — treatments such as hypnosis or acupuncture are, as you will discover, not compatible with this approach.

Is there a right time to stop smoking? Only *you* will know when that moment will be. It's obviously best not to choose a time of great stress. If you use this technique correctly, the process of stopping will require much of your attention to begin with. You will need to spend some time studying this book and thinking about what you are doing. So, if you have something unusual and particularly demanding coming up soon, such as exams, it's better to wait until after they are over before you go ahead with stopping smoking. If you are in an unusually traumatic situation, for any reason, it will also be better to wait a while.

If you have recently stopped taking some other drug you have been dependent on, whether prescribed or not, it will be advisable to wait a while before stopping smoking, *especially* if you increased your level of smoking in the process. You will have transferred at least some of your dependency over to cigarettes, and you may be taking on too much at once to try stopping smoking as well. If you want to stop taking another drug but have not yet done so, then it's fine to stop smoking first: just deal with each problem one at a time.

Apart from these circumstances, the sooner you stop, the better it will be for you. You are the only one who can decide whether you have a really justifiable reason to wait or if you are just making excuses.

It might be a good idea, right now, to write on the inside front cover the date you bought or started to read this book. Then, if you pick it up again much later on, and you still haven't got around to stopping, you may get stunned into action!

In other words   *JEAN*

What I want to say to people reading this book is don't worry about it, just read it — it makes sense. Even if you don't manage to stop, you will always remember key things which, when you do give up, will be invaluable.

I had no expectations when I started the course. I had smoked for nearly thirty years. I had tried acupuncture and hypnotherapy, both of which only helped me to cut down for a brief time. I smoked thirty a day which I enjoyed, and really never wanted to give up. I hoped for a miracle and a magic wand, which I also knew did not exist.

The most important thing to learn was to stop smoking for myself. I spend my life doing things for others (as most women do) and didn't think to do something for me. This has changed my life.

2 THE NATURE OF ADDICTION

'A cigarette is the perfect type of a perfect
pleasure. It is exquisite, and it leaves one
unsatisfied. What more can one want?'

Oscar Wilde, *The Picture of Dorian Gray*

WHEN I was a smoker, I didn't think of myself as addicted. I just thought I was smoking, like most other people I knew. It was only when I stopped smoking and was seriously trying to stay stopped that I began to realise that I had, in fact, been in the grip of an addiction.

Often smokers deny they are addicted even though they smoke daily for years. You hear them say: 'I'm not addicted — I enjoy smoking', as if the two were mutually exclusive. These are the smokers who claim they can stop easily any time they want to. But, you may notice, they don't stay stopped.

Other smokers are all too eager to admit to being addicted because they use that to justify their smoking. Being addicted is their way of explaining — both to themselves and others — why they continue to smoke, with the implication, of course, that there is nothing they can do about it.

Then there are smokers who take such a severe moral stance towards any drug addiction that they are very reluctant to think of themselves in that way. These people have a stereotyped image of the 'drug addict' as a deviant and dangerous character. Each drug addiction has its own unique qualities, but just because a drug is legal doesn't mean that it isn't just as addictive as illegal drugs. Millions of people have become dependent on relatively socially acceptable drugs such as alcohol, nicotine and caffeine.

So what is an addiction? Is it in your mind or in your body? And what can you do about it? Understanding addiction, and especially this one, is your first step.

Nicotine in Your Body

Here is an important question to consider. If you have found stopping smoking to be intolerable, or if you are able to stop but find you keep going back, is this because your body has developed a need for nicotine, a physical dependency that must be satisfied at any cost? Let's start by looking at what happens in your body and in your mind when you smoke.

First and foremost, smoking a cigarette is a way of administering the drug nicotine. Some gets absorbed slowly through the inside of your mouth but most of it is inhaled into your lungs where it is very rapidly taken into your blood stream. It is then carried in the blood all round your body, and especially to your brain.

Many people think that the reason they smoke is to maintain the amount of nicotine in their blood. This, they think, is what drives them to light cigarette after cigarette. However, if you carefully examine your own experience of smoking, I think you will see there is actually something else far more important to you.

Look at it this way. What if, unknown to you, somebody, somehow put nicotine into your blood stream. Would you really have any way of knowing it was there? And, even more important, would you then lose your interest in smoking cigarettes?

I think you would still want to smoke, for the same reason that you sometimes still want to light up another cigarette even when you've just finished one. For the same reason that people still crave cigarettes while they are chewing nicotine gum. A number of scientific experiments demonstrate this point.

In one, smokers who had abstained from smoking overnight were given an intravenous infusion. On one occasion it contained saline and on another it contained sufficient nicotine to reach concentrations in the blood stream comparable to those achieved by smoking. They were not told which was which. 'Subjects were unable to discriminate between conditions. At the end of the infusion there was no difference in self-reported desire to smoke, nor in latency to lighting up a cigarette when this was permitted. Complete nicotine replacement was therefore not accompanied by complete suppression of smoking behaviour.' (1)

These smokers still wanted to smoke — and did smoke — regardless of whether or not they had adequate amounts of nicotine in their blood stream.

The Buzz

Does this mean that nicotine is irrelevant? Certainly not! The point I am making is that when you smoke a cigarette, it's not so much the amount of nicotine in your blood that you want or think you need: you can hardly tell it's there.

What you really want are the sensations you get, for just a few seconds, when a dose of nicotine *is entering* your body. You know the feeling. For a few seconds your heart races and you feel a dizzy kind of intoxication. Extra adrenalin runs through your body. It's a feeling of excitement, a very brief 'lift' or 'high'. It's a nicotine buzz.

In the experiment I just mentioned, the nicotine was delivered gradually, over one hour. If it had been administered quickly the subjects would have been aware of it and it would have felt to them like smoking, delivering a buzz and thus satisfying their desire to smoke. (2)

If you have ever tried using nicotine gum you will know what I'm talking about. It delivers the nicotine too slowly to be truly satisfying. Some people can get a very mild buzz from it, and can even get hooked on it, just as some get hooked on other slow delivery methods, like non-inhaling pipe and cigar smokers. Nicotine in your blood, even if delivered very gradually, will make your heart beat a little bit faster, among other things, but the effect it has is much more subtle. *For the vast majority of cigarette smokers, the buzz is the most important thing, and you only get that by a sudden, rapidly absorbed dose of nicotine.*

Unfortunately this increased heart rate isn't real energy — otherwise athletes would smoke during marathons. It's a false stimulation, and like all artificial highs it's immediately followed by a depressed state. To make matters worse, cigarette smoke includes many poisons too, so although the heart is beating faster there is less energy-producing oxygen in the blood. This is why most smokers find they have more energy when they stop.

Getting it Right

As you know, the buzz is stronger when you haven't smoked for a while. It is at its best when a dose of nicotine rapidly enters a brain and body that contain relatively low levels of nicotine. Like the first cigarette of the day, for example.

But the balance has to be right, because for most smokers, if you smoke too infrequently the sensations are too strong and can even make you nauseous. So you need to keep smoking a certain amount in order to maintain some tolerance.

On the other hand, if you smoke too frequently you don't get enough buzz. This is the bad news: the buzz is subject to 'rapid acute tolerance'. This means that after the first puff of the first cigarette you've had in a while, you get a much weaker sensation. Quite probably, most of the cigarettes you smoke in a day don't manage to deliver a good buzz, but you keep trying anyway. I know I did.

This is the reason why smokers can still have a desire to smoke even though they have got plenty of nicotine in their body. For some smokers there are times when smoking a cigarette doesn't satisfy the desire, so that they still feel a craving while actually smoking a cigarette. That's because they are still wanting the buzz but just not getting it. For some this can develop into chain-smoking, which is a continuous and largely unsuccessful attempt to satisfy the desire to smoke.

It's a never-ending tease, delivering the prize just often enough to keep you interested. You try to get that buzz feeling as often as you can, waiting in between cigarettes for as long as you can for the nicotine level to drop a bit, so that it feels strong enough when the nicotine goes in. This is why cigarettes are particularly enjoyable after physical exercise and after a meal: the nicotine level has been brought down, giving you a better buzz when you smoke.

Need or Desire?

The crucial point to understand about the buzz is that it is desired and pursued, consciously or unconsciously, *regardless of how much nicotine you have in your body*. The experience of a client of mine illustrates this vital point.

Malcolm, in his mid-forties, came to my classes recently and told me that six months earlier, quite out of the blue, he had suffered a major heart attack and had been taken to hospital for emergency surgery.

He stayed in the hospital for a week, and although he had been smoking forty cigarettes a day for thirty years, he hardly even thought of cigarettes while he was there. He told me he didn't feel any withdrawal symptoms and didn't have any particular interest in smoking at all. Of course, he was under some kind of sedation for the first day or two which would have masked any symptoms he might otherwise have had, but not for the rest of that week.

Then he told me what happened on the day he was discharged. As he walked away from the hospital, he passed a pub and thought how nice it would be to have a beer and a cigarette. So he did, and then he resumed smoking his two packets of cigarettes a day.

The point is that when he went into that pub, it wasn't because his body suddenly wanted or needed nicotine at that precise instant. His body didn't want or need it the day before in the hospital and it didn't then. The reason he smoked was because of the *thought*: 'Wouldn't it be nice to have a cigarette?', which he then acted on. It was a thought he hadn't had for a few days because of the circumstances he was in.

There is an important question here. If Malcolm had not smoked at that time, what would he then have experienced? The answer is that he would have begun the real process of stopping smoking, long after the nicotine had left his body. He would have started a process which is mental, and not physical at all.

Malcolm went through the physical stage of withdrawal and didn't even notice it, but he never did go through his mental withdrawal: and this is why he didn't stay stopped.

The Taste

You may think the reason Malcolm smoked is simply because he enjoyed the taste of tobacco, but this is an effect rather than a cause. Any addict will make positive associations with whatever is directly connected to their addiction. Heroin addicts actually get some satisfaction from injecting themselves with plain water when they can't get heroin. Psychologists call this secondary conditioning.

As a smoker, you develop a special fondness for the taste of tobacco because you associate it with the buzz of getting your nicotine fix. Sometimes you do enjoy the taste, but if you only tasted tobacco and never got any buzz at all you would only feel frustrated. I would suggest that the cigarettes you most enjoy — probably only a few in a day — are those that deliver the strongest buzz.

You don't make a positive association with herbal cigarettes because they don't deliver the goods. They don't satisfy the addiction to nicotine. The whole experience of pleasure: the taste and smell, the sensation of the smoke in your throat, the feel and appearance of cigarettes, including your brand logo, is bound up in your mind with the one essential component: the buzz.

Physically, nicotine enters the body producing a brief, excited, dizzy sensation, as well as making your heart beat faster for a few seconds. Then, *mentally*, you think: 'That was nice!' or: 'That was helpful!'

The Crutch

'That was helpful!' expresses the common belief that nicotine makes a valuable, even essential, contribution to your life. This belief takes various forms, and you may hold one or more of them yourself:

□ You believe that, without nicotine, you will not be as mentally alert, as able to concentrate, or make decisions.

□ You think you will not function as well physically, have as much energy or stamina, be able to relax completely, get going in the morning, get to sleep at night or digest your food properly.

☐ You fear you won't be able to control your moods, stay calm or keep anger or depresssion at bay.

☐ You are concerned you won't be able to enjoy yourself socially.

These beliefs always look very convincing: they have to be in order to fool you. You would not think, for example, that smoking enables you to leap tall buildings in a single bound. That's too absurd.

The beliefs that smokers develop have to be believable, even containing fragments of truth. What happens is you take those fragments and go on to ascribe qualities and capabilities to the nicotine buzz far beyond what it actually achieves chemically. After years of believing these misconceptions, eventually cigarettes are thought of as an indispensable crutch.

Discovering what is and isn't true about this so-called crutch in your life is part of what's involved in stopping smoking. In another chapter, *Why Smoking Seems to Help*, we will disentangle the truth from the illusion behind each of these beliefs.

Another word for addiction is dependency: you believe you are dependent on nicotine in order to function as well as you do mentally, physically and emotionally. But no human body actually needs nicotine: your belief that you need it — your dependency — is a product of your mind.

The Object of Desire

Many smokers, of course, believe themselves to be physically dependent because of the presence of physical withdrawal symptoms whenever they stop smoking. They think they are in for a distressing experience caused by an inevitable, chemical reaction to the absence of nicotine in their system.

The familiar nightmare stories include: tension, restlessness, anxiety, loss of concentration, loss of sleep, hunger, severe mood changes and, last but not least, a dreadful craving for a cigarette. It is, however, a critical mistake to put these distressing effects all down to physical chemistry.

One way to begin to understand the real cause is to realise that most of these symptoms can be experienced equally strongly in other situations, not connected with chemical withdrawal of any kind. They are, in fact, the product of particular *states of mind*.

Even the desire to smoke is a product of the mind, created by the memory of the nicotine buzz. It can be hard to understand this, because the desire to smoke is experienced by most people as a strong, *physically* uncomfortable sensation. Many describe the craving as a hollow emptiness, a hunger or a void, which they can locate in their bodies. Because it is a physical experience, most people ascribe a *physical* cause, and the cause they think of is: insufficient nicotine!

But look at another kind of desire. You can create very physical sensations of sexual desire simply by bringing certain things to mind, like an erotic fantasy, or an erotic memory. The desire to smoke arises in a similar way, except that the object of desire in this case is the nicotine buzz.

Physical Withdrawal

This doesn't mean, however, that everything about stopping smoking is entirely in the mind. Smoking does involve your body, and when you stop there certainly are things that will happen on a purely physical level.

There is a mild physical withdrawal, which is the result of an inevitable process of change that your body will go through. Along with nicotine, there are at least 4,000 different chemicals, many of which are poisonous, in cigarette smoke which get absorbed into your body. So when you stop, you go through a process of recovery: a detoxification. If you have ever had a hangover from drinking alcohol, then you have experienced physical withdrawal from a drug.

If you have done a great deal of smoking, it may feel for a couple of days after stopping like you are coming down with a bad cold. That's about as nasty as it gets. It's very temporary and not at all dramatic or intolerable. It's actually a cleaning out process and therefore the beginning of an improved state of health.

After you stop, the nicotine leaves your body. It is eliminated in the same way as any other toxin in the blood stream and, according to medical researchers who have measured nicotine levels in blood samples, it leaves the body in less than twenty-four hours. (3)

Physical damage and residues from many years of smoking will, of course, take longer to rectify, but that is nothing to do with the effects of a drug. If your lungs take a while to clean themselves out, that's just a consequence of having stopped. It's not part of what's involved in being able to stop.

As far as the physical elimination of nicotine is concerned, you don't need to do anything about it. Your body will take care of itself, all by itself.

Addiction in Your Mind

Even after you have stopped smoking, and all traces of nicotine have left your body, the memory of the nicotine buzz still persists. And it is how you handle that desire for the buzz that primarily affects your experience of stopping smoking.

In fact, what you have done is to form a *psychological attachment to the physical sensations* you got from smoking. The nicotine has an effect on your body, but it's your mind that desires the effect. It's your mind that believes you need nicotine. And it's your mind that registers satisfaction when you get your buzz, or objects in the most dramatic ways if the desire is not satisfied. *And it's your mind that decides whether you'll go on smoking or choose to stop.*

Physical withdrawal doesn't determine whether you will be successful at stopping smoking. It's your mind that determines whether or not you will go through that experience, and whether or not you go back to smoking, long after the physical changes are over.

When you stop, after some minor and temporary physical changes, your body will be much healthier and happier, since you are no longer putting so much poison into it. But your mind will not be happy because, unlike your body, it does not make the change to not smoking automatically. It remains the mind of a smoker, but it's the mind of a smoker who isn't smoking. And that inevitably sets up a conflict.

All this is the process of *mental withdrawal,* and unless it's dealt with correctly you may very well be smoking again weeks or months after the *physical withdrawal* is over.

If you are still not convinced, it may help to look at other addictions which have nothing to do with the ingestion of a drug. People can become addicted to a whole variety of things, such as gambling, computer games, exercise or food. These people will experience very similar symptoms when they stop, such as intense compulsions or cravings, feelings of deprivation, anger, irritability, anxiety, depression and fear.

You Can Work it Out

I am not saying that it's all in your mind, therefore you are imagining all your problems and they don't really exist. The problems are real, and so is the addiction.

What I am saying is that in order for you to successfully stop smoking and stay stopped, to really take control of this addiction, you will need to change what is going on in your mind. And you can't do that by just waiting for it to change: you need to work at it. *It requires your active participation.* This book will show you what to do and why and how to do it. But nobody can change your thinking for you.

An addiction is held in place by an elaborate system of deceptions. If you have been deceiving yourself in this way for a long time, it will probably all look very real to you.

What stopping smoking — and staying stopped — is all about is discovering the truth. Once you have done that, it's not so easy to get conned again. If you are willing to put effort into reading, thinking and questioning, you have every chance of real success this time.

In other words   *DAVID*

I had struggled for years with starting and stopping smoking, kidding myself that because I knew I could stop any time I was really in control.

I stopped after my mother died of cancer with a firm intention to stay off. I went back to it a year later and smoked for five years before I stopped again. This time I relapsed after a few months. Then I stopped again, and got back when I allowed myself to smoke a roll-up on the principle that they were different in some way! I was back on twenty-a-day within a few weeks.

Gillian's course (five and a half years ago) showed me that you can't play with an addiction – it always wins! Now I see it as something with its own power and I know now how to experience an addictive desire, and how to stand outside it without denying it, or feeling denied.

References

1. Jarvis, M. *Nicotine Replacement: A Critical Evaluation* (1988) p.146.
    In another experiment, volunteer smokers were given pills to take regularly during a normal smoking day and, at the same time, were asked to keep a record of when they smoked. They were unaware of the content of the pills, which were identified only by the day and time they were to be taken. On some days the smokers took nothing but sugar pills, but on other days they took doses of nicotine equivalent to that ingested by smoking. On average, they smoked twenty-four cigarettes on the days they were taking the sugar pills and twenty-two cigarettes on the nicotine days.
    Jarvik, Glick and Nakamura Inhibition of cigarette smoking by orally administered nicotine. *Clinical Pharmacology and Therapeutics* (1970) 11:574-76.
2. Injections of nicotine were given to thirty-five volunteers. 'Smokers almost invariably thought the sensation pleasant, and given an adequate dose, were disinclined to smoke for a time thereafter. After a course of eighty injections of nicotine, an injection was preferred to a cigarette.'
    Johnston, L. Tobacco Smoking and Nicotine. *The Lancet* (1942) p.742.
3. From the last cigarette smoked, the amount of nicotine in the blood stream drops by half every two hours. After twelve hours, very little nicotine is left.
    Benowitz, N., Jacob, P., Jones, R. and Rosenberg, J. Interindividual variability in the metabolism and cardiovascular effects of nicotine in man. *Journal of Pharmacology and Experimental Therapeutics* (1982) 221:368-372.

3 THE DESIRE TO SMOKE

'Tobacco, divine, rare, superexcellent tobacco . . . a sovereign remedy to all diseases. But, as it is commonly abused by most men, which take it as tinkers do ale, 'tis a plague, a mischief, a violent purger of goods, lands, health; hellish, devilish, and damned tobacco, the ruin and overthrow of body and soul.'

Robert Burton, *Anatomy of Melancholy*

WHENEVER a thought crosses your mind which leads to the lighting of a cigarette, you have experienced the desire to smoke. Sometimes it feels like an urge, a craving or a compulsion to smoke. Sometimes, you just think to yourself that you fancy a cigarette, or that smoking would help you in some way. So you light one. As a smoker, you are continuously feeding and satisfying that desire by smoking cigarette after cigarette after cigarette.

A Part of Your Life

The desire to smoke may be associated with virtually any situation or circumstance in your life. This is a feature of all addictions, especially smoking: the conditioned reflex that the scientist Pavlov first demonstrated with his dog. Pavlov rang a bell every time he fed his dog, and after a while the dog would salivate whenever it heard the bell, thinking food was on the way. Just like Pavlov's dog, some smokers actually salivate for a cigarette on hearing the telephone ring. You train yourself, over and over, to expect a cigarette (a nicotine buzz), especially on certain cues.

I'm sure you would have no difficulty in identifying all kinds of things that you associate with smoking. This is why smoking is thought of as a habit, because it's so integrated into your life. Just think of all the situations that apply to you: taking a break, finishing a meal, making a decision, concentrating on a demanding task, or just completing one, answering the phone, sitting in a traffic jam, drinking coffee, having a beer, seeing another smoker light a cigarette and smelling the smoke. You will also have conditioned yourself to expect to smoke whenever you feel strong emotions: especially anger and frustration, but also sadness, boredom, anxiety, embarrassment, and even triumph, joy and excitement.

The list is endless. Just about anything that happens, or doesn't happen, in a smoker's life can result in the idea of smoking a cigarette.

Fortunately, it is not essential to identify all these cues, especially since it could be quite an insignificant thought or simply a shift in your thinking, like: 'What shall I do now?' (Answer: 'I'll have a cigarette!') The main point here is that the desire to smoke, the expectation of smoking, is triggered in your mind repeatedly. Something happens and you think, automatically, that smoking a cigarette would be helpful and/or enjoyable. So you light a cigarette.

If you've been smoking regularly for a number of years, this thought will be so familiar to you that it can often go unnoticed, such as when you suddenly realise you have a half-smoked cigarette in your hand, with absolutely no recollection of having lit it.

But even though you may not be aware of it there is *always* something in your mind that initiates the lighting of a cigarette. There has to be some thought that tells your hand to pick up a cigarette and light it. This thought is your desire to smoke: you just aren't conscious of it at times.

And, if you have ever stopped smoking for any length of time, the reason you went back to smoking was because you had the same old desire to light a cigarette, and you did so. Often people say they went back to smoking because of certain circumstances, such as an argument or an accident. But what actually happened was this: the situation triggered a conditioned reflex, a desire to smoke, which you then satisfied. This may seem obvious, but it's important to see the whole sequence of events: first the situation, then the desire, *then* the action.

If you smoke forty cigarettes a day, then at least forty

times a day you are experiencing — and satisfying — your desire to smoke. Sometimes you enjoy them and sometimes you don't. Sometimes they seem helpful and sometimes they are a nuisance. *Always*, you are smoking not because events somehow magically make you reach out and light up a cigarette, but because they act as a trigger to your addictive desire.

Why do you have this desire to smoke? The answer is simply and entirely because of all the smoking you have done in the past. Smoking is 'learned behaviour'. And you have reinforced your desire to smoke with every cigarette you ever smoked. You satisfy the desire, and you reinforce it at the same time.

If you had only ever smoked ten cigarettes, then your desire to smoke would only have been reinforced ten times. Unfortunately, people who have only smoked ten cigarettes usually aren't motivated to stop smoking. So they go on reinforcing the desire until they have smoked as many as a quarter of a million cigarettes before they really get serious about trying to stop.

Some smokers set up rules for themselves, or go along with rules set up by others, and don't smoke in certain circumstances. For instance, some people never, ever smoke in certain rooms, such as the bedroom. Others never smoke before breakfast or in their cars and many never smoke during some work situations, such as while teaching or interviewing people. In these situations, the desire to smoke doesn't usually get triggered because the association is never made. But you are certainly smoking as habitually and addictively all the rest of the time.

As we discussed in the last chapter, a desire to smoke is a thought that comes to your mind, regardless of how much nicotine there happens to be in your body at the time. Your body doesn't need more nicotine just because you're on a coffee break. Your body's nicotine level doesn't fall danger-ously low the moment a friend comes to visit and lights up in your kitchen. What happens is that you are reminded of smoking when break-time comes along, or the smoking friend shows up, and you anticipate another opportunity to get your nicotine buzz.

Non-smokers and Ex-smokers

What you have done is this: you have trained yourself to expect a cigarette, especially on certain cues, and you have reinforced that training thousands of times over.

There are people, of course, who never did that. They never smoked, never reinforced the behaviour and so the idea of smoking doesn't occur to them. They are non-smokers, and they often have a hard time understanding why anyone smokes at all. If they get a piece of bad news, they just get upset. They don't get upset and then reach for a cigarette, like you do. Smoking simply doesn't occur to them, not because they were born fundamentally superior in some crucial way, or because their lives are especially easy, but because they never chose to become smokers and establish that particular conditioning in the first place.

The big question here is: is it possible for a smoker to become a non-smoker? Is there a way to stop smoking and never think of smoking again? Can you undo the years of conditioning so that, for example, when the phone rings, you just answer it?

For the great majority of smokers, this looks like the ideal — and perhaps only — solution, but the truth is that once this conditioning has been deeply ingrained, there is no way to magically erase it. It has been too frequently reinforced, too thoroughly integrated into your life and mind. Brace yourself for the bad news: some desire to smoke is always likely to recur. However much you may want to forget all about smoking after you have stopped, it's impossible for you to become someone who has never smoked. As a smoker, you cannot become a non-smoker. You can, however, choose to become an ex-smoker. This distinction is crucial.

The good news is that once you have stopped smoking, the conditioning begins to fade because you are no longer reinforcing it. The sooner you stop smoking and the longer you stay stopped, the more it fades. More about this later.

Remembering the Buzz

Once you have become a smoker, you will always have a memory of being a smoker. If you can remember things you did only once, ten or twenty years ago, it's really very likely that you will remember something you did many times, every day, for most of your adult life.

But remembering what it's like to smoke is more than an ordinary recollection, because the nicotine buzz has been etched deep into your memory. It's a memory of the effects of a drug. This memory persists. If you stop smoking, it will fade gradually, but the old conditioning never totally disappears. What this means is that, as an ex-smoker, you will at times still experience some desire to smoke as an automatic reaction, especially on those most significant cues: after a meal, when feeling strong emotions, when in the company of other smokers, to name a few of the most common examples.

This is probably the last thing you want to hear, but, as with any problem, it works much better to tackle the facts rather than pretend they don't exist just because you don't like them.

Most smokers definitely do not like the idea that they may continue to feel the desire to smoke after they have stopped. This is why most stopping-smoking methods are aimed at helping you to avoid this unpleasant reality. You may have tried such a method and found that it helped you to stop — but not to stay stopped.

In the short term, it's relatively easy to focus on the disgusting and dangerous aspects of smoking, so that you are able to fend off the desire to have a cigarette. But it's only a matter of time before that argument wears a bit thin. Your memory of the addiction comes back — you want that buzz — and you are smoking again.

A great many smokers, after many failed attempts to stop, have finally come to realise this truth; that the desire doesn't entirely leave them. Unfortunately, what they then conclude is that they will not be able to stay stopped for very long. So many smokers fail at stopping smoking over and over again because they are hoping to rid themselves of the addictive desire. *If success for you means not wanting to smoke ever again, then failure is inevitable!*

There is, however, a way out. And here is the key. Just because you feel a desire to smoke, it doesn't mean that you *have* to smoke. You can learn how to handle this desire

without ending up smoking. You may think, at first, that
this is quite impossible, but it is an approach which has
proved its long-term success and if you are prepared to read
on, every step of how to do this will become clear.

I have taught and counselled hundreds of smokers over
the last ten years, with excellent long-term results: over
seventy-five per cent of people who complete my course are
still not smoking one year later. *To be successful in the long
term you will stay stopped not because you have lost the
desire to smoke, but because you have learned how to
handle it.* That's how I have managed to stay stopped for
the last ten years, and you can do it too. It takes some time
and effort to begin with, but it's possible.

There are just two main obstacles to learning how to
handle the desire to smoke and so successfully stop
smoking. The first is a sense of deprivation, and the second
is resisting the desire.

Feeling Deprived

If you've ever stopped smoking in the past and experienced
a sense of deprivation, you may also have experienced an
aggravated and probably intolerable desire to smoke. Believing you are deprived makes things seem a hundred times
worse: you panic, get exaggerated cravings, and feel
depressed, hostile and martyred.

*But you can experience a desire to smoke without having
a sense of deprivation.* You may never have thought that
possible, but Chapters Four and Five will show you how.

Resisting the Desire

The truth is that, as a smoker, you are faced with two
different options. One is to continue smoking. The other is
to learn how to deal with your desire to smoke, which
enables you to stop and stay stopped.

For many smokers, both these options look lousy: a
lifetime of smoking looks grim, but having an unsatisfied
desire to smoke doesn't look like much fun either. In fact,
once you learn how to deal with the desire properly it very

quickly becomes easy to handle. But, if you don't know how to do this, the best you can hope for is that it will somehow go away if you wait long enough.

If you have ever made any attempt to stop smoking before, you probably know what I'm talking about. It's very likely that you often felt a strong desire to smoke, but tried to ignore it, and at times when that was impossible, you fought it.

This is unfortunate because, in fact, much of the difficulty in stopping smoking comes not from feeling the desire to smoke, *but from not wanting that feeling to be there.* It is because you are setting yourself up in conflict with your desire to smoke that you experience the greatest difficulty at this stage. Many symptoms of tension and anxiety which are thought of as withdrawal symptoms are a product of this conflict. Nervous energy, nausea, head, jaw, neck, shoulder and stomach aches, clenched teeth and white knuckles are all expressions of a fight going on inside you. It is you, fighting your desire, not wanting to feel it. You may not deliberately fight it; this resistance is usually automatic.

You may also feel a certain amount of fear, because while you are in conflict with the desire, you are always on the verge of giving in to it. You may feel overwhelmed by it, or *fear* that you will be overwhelmed by it eventually. The fear makes you fight it even more, so you end up feeling like a battlefield. After a while, when the fighting wears you out, you return to smoking, regretting another failure.

There is, however, another solution to all this. It is highly effective and it's something that can easily become part of your everyday life. And it has to do with accepting the desire, accepting that it is there, and not preparing to fight against it. The desire to smoke is as inevitable as a brick wall. When you stop banging your head against it, wishing it wasn't there, it won't hurt so much!

There's another problem that comes from resisting the desire to smoke. If you think you should get rid of the desire, you may be able to create the illusion that you have done just that. This is a trap that can make it easy to stop, but is guaranteed to take you back to smoking later on.

At the Back of Your Mind

Most of the time, people who stop smoking try to resist the desire to smoke. Some will even be able to shut out the urge completely, so that they don't feel it at all. Here's a definition of repression from *A Primer Of Freudian Psychology*:

> Repression forces a dangerous memory, idea or perception out of consciousness and sets up a barrier against any form of motor discharge [physical emotion or feeling].

Repression is a coping mechanism and can even be essential to our survival. As one very practical example, if you run from danger and sprain a leg, the pain is repressed and only becomes apparent when you reach safety.

Repressing your emotions is also a way of coping with difficult situations. You may repress your anger when an outburst will create trouble. You may repress sadness in order to put on a brave face over some tragedy.

For most smokers, repression of the desire to smoke is the sole mechanism they use to stop smoking. And they are often encouraged to do so, by a broad variety of techniques and books on the subject. Sometimes the advice is directed towards getting smoking off your mind: keep yourself busy, change your routines and avoid situations that might make you want to smoke. If you think about smoking, distract yourself quickly so that you don't get tempted.

Some people like to boast about being able to stop without experiencing any desire to smoke at all, or maybe only a little. This just means that they are repressing very effectively. Some people repress things easily, some people don't. It doesn't necessarily mean that you are less addicted. If you stopped smoking in the past and thought it was easy, then you probably did it by repressing. In Chapter Two we looked at the story of Malcolm who completely repressed his desire to smoke for a whole week while in hospital. He is not uncommon: many smokers are able to repress for days or weeks at a time, especially when they are ill or in unfamiliar surroundings. But even if you can keep it up for days or weeks, it is rarely possible to repress for ever.

Many smokers are quite unable to repress at all. And a

smoker becomes less able to repress the desire to smoke as the years go by. So a smoker who can repress effectively after five years of smoking, and so stop smoking for periods of time, will most likely not be able to after twenty years of smoking. If you are relying on repression as a way to stop smoking, it is just a question of time before you feel a strong enough desire and start again.

There are a number of techniques which help smokers to repress their desire. Most forms of acupuncture and hypnosis are attempts to do that. So, too, is aversion therapy. If the technique represses effectively, then it will, of course, have a high short-term success rate. Let's take a closer look at aversion techniques, as it is very likely you have been trying this approach, without necessarily realising it.

A Filthy Mess

Most people, whether they smoke or not, have some adverse thoughts about smoking. Certainly people who have never smoked often hate everything about it: all they see is that it smells foul, creates mess, and is bad for your health.

Many smokers also find smoking revolting, at least on some occasions. The morning after a party, for example, they can feel sickened physically and mentally by all the cigarettes they got through the night before. Then they won't have any desire to smoke at all, or a very minor one that can easily be ignored.

One well-known aversion technique makes use of this phenomenon by instructing the smoker to smoke rapidly and excessively, focusing on how much the smoke hurts and burns and makes you feel ill. Another technique is to deliver electric shocks as you smoke, and a slightly less drastic one is to snap a rubber band round your wrist. The idea is to create an association between smoking and pain. An aversion can also be developed simply by repeating, over and over again, how evil, filthy and useless smoking is.

In all cases, the intention is the same: to put you off wanting to smoke, and so over-ride the desire for a cigarette. Then, whenever you think of smoking, or whenever someone offers you a cigarette, your reaction is meant to be one of disgust and revulsion.

It's one way of stopping, and for a few people it can work in the long term as well. You have probably met the kind of ex-smoker who makes a great deal of this, making the point over and over again about how smoking is dirty and repulsive and smelly and unhealthy. They are acting out their own aversion, reinforcing it by talking about it.

So what's the problem? Well, in order to be effective in the long term, the aversion has to be absolute and unequivocal. And the problem with that is that the human mind is complex and often contradictory (any human mind, not just yours!). Most people find it impossible to remain so utterly single-minded, especially when it comes to an addiction. The hung-over smoker mentioned before is thoroughly sickened, all morning, by the idea of smoking. But as the hang-over fades, so does the aversion. The smoker begins to feel like smoking again and is puffing away as usual by the end of the day.

You can work very hard at developing your aversion, but it is inevitable that you will also have some good memories of smoking. The addictive desire will come back to you — and an addiction means that you have a compulsion to do whatever it is you are addicted to. Therefore, it is entirely possible to be totally convinced, at one moment, that smoking is the most loathsome and foul thing on earth, and yet, moments later, to be completely enveloped in a powerful desire to smoke, believing that smoking a cigarette would be enjoyable, exciting and generally life-enhancing. Both these extremes co-exist in the mind of the smoker and they continue to do so after the smoker has stopped.

It is, of course, entirely realistic to have adverse thoughts about smoking. That's probably what makes you want to stop smoking in the first place. The truth is that smoking *does* burn your throat, it *does* make you feel ill and it *does* smell foul. (By the way, if you are unwilling to acknowledge these facts at all, it's because you are terrified of feeling deprived, as Chapter Four will explain.) It's fine to remember these things, but don't expect them to eliminate your desire to smoke. An aversion to smoking which results in

repression of the addictive desire is usually a very temporary way of stopping.

Sooner or later, you will experience the return of your
desire to smoke. It may be when you are under stress, or
while relaxing on holiday. It may be when you feel
miserable and alone, or thoroughly enjoying yourself at a
party, surrounded by friends.

If you want to stop smoking and stay stopped this time,
you are much more likely to succeed if you learn to live
with that reality. It isn't your aversion that will keep you
from smoking, but your ability to deal with your desire to
smoke.

Repression Doesn't Work

There are far more problems associated with repression,
however, than the simple fact that most people can't keep
it up for ever.

First of all there are the extraordinary lengths some
people go to in order to reach the impossible goal of ridding
themselves of their desire for a smoke. Avoiding anything
that might make you want to smoke, including other
smokers in both work and social situations, soon becomes
an impractical and inconvenient charade. Keeping yourself
occupied at *all* times also turns out to be impossible.

Clients of mine have told me all sorts of weird and
wonderful strategies they have devised on previous desperate attempts to quit. One woman who lived in the country
told me that every time she wanted to smoke, she went
outside and ran as fast as she could all the way round her
house, screaming loudly. Another said that for a while he
tried smoking only while he was standing on his head, the
theory being that by breaking down all other cues to smoke,
he would only want to smoke when upside down. Because
this would happen so rarely, eventually he would be free
from the desire to smoke!

Needless to say, both these approaches failed, which is
why these smokers ended up at my course. I'd like to add
that both have now stopped and have not smoked since.
Their success this time was the result of learning a

completely different way of dealing with their desire to smoke.

A more serious problem with repression can be understood when you realise that the desire to smoke is an energy, a physical force not unlike emotions such as anger and grief. It is now widely accepted that chronic repression of emotions leads to physical illness. Dr Bernie Siegel puts it very clearly in his excellent book on this subject, *Love, Medicine And Miracles*:

> If a person deals with anger or despair when they first appear, illness need not occur. When we don't deal with our emotional needs, we set ourselves up for physical illness.

When you repress any part of a natural process of change, the repressed experience doesn't somehow vanish, but simply gets moved into a part of your subconscious mind, so that you are temporarily unaware of it. With stopping smoking, the effect of repressing your desire shows up in symptoms like hunger, loss of sleep and poor concentration.

Defusing the Bomb

The irony is that ex-smokers can feel quite confident when they are repressing their desire to smoke. It seems to them that they have their problem under control and that they have truly broken the addiction this time. It's a very common and attractive error to see the absence of addictive desire as a sign of having succeeded.

But repression is, at best, a temporary way of stopping smoking. It's like sitting on a time-bomb: the only question is when it will explode. And when it does, you can be smoking before you have even a chance to know what is happening. If you do not have your mind trained to deal with the desire, there is no way you can control it.

Repressive techniques will be effective for a few people, but they don't work for most people in the long term. (1)

The technique this book describes takes an entirely different approach. It is based on the fact that the desire to smoke cannot be completely and permanently eliminated. Therefore, you either continue to try avoiding it for as long as you can, in which case you are likely to end up smoking eventually. Or, you can learn how to face up to it, and deal with it. If you do that, you can defuse the time-bomb.

It may seem more difficult in the beginning; but you will have no fear of the bomb going off later on.

Real Control

When you learn how to deal with your desire to smoke, you have every chance of success in stopping and staying stopped for good. You don't fight it, you don't try to make it go away, and you don't expect it to go away. You remember that *repression of the desire temporarily removes the problem; it doesn't solve it*. In fact, it's only when you accept the desire to smoke that you are really in control. The desire will diminish in time, but the first thing is to expect it and accept it. It's not a sign of weakness or impending failure: it's a perfectly normal aspect of being an ex-smoker.

Once you have stopped, the urge to smoke will happen less and less often. But it's not just the infrequency of desire that will keep you from smoking; it's that you will have learned how to deal with it.

You will be able to see it for what it is, separate it from whatever else is happening, and make a choice about what you are going to do.

In other words   **GILL**

Although I wanted to stop smoking, I had severe doubts that I could. When I started the course I was on about thirty a day. I enjoyed some cigarettes very much; the majority I did not and I felt uncomfortable being so tied to something that most of the time was a habit rather than a pleasure. I realised I had completely lost control over my smoking.

During the course, because of my misgivings, I think I was unconsciously resisting the technique. I frequently felt cross and couldn't believe it could possibly work. However, I followed the instructions and guide-lines. The first few days were very difficult but, unlike the time I had stopped smoking before, the grim period passed within two weeks.

To me, the most important aspect of the technique was that it allowed me to feel the desire to smoke and not to feel frightened of that. This permission is, in fact, one's eventual freedom. The desire to smoke stops being something to be terrified of, to dread, and to want to suppress. Once that awful pressure comes off, one quietly stops smoking.

A year on I feel quite secure around cigarettes and other smokers. They don't bother me. I don't feel I want to boast that I've stopped smoking; I just accept and am glad that it has happened. For me it has been a 'quiet revolution' and because it has been a quiet one, I feel confident that it will last.

References

1. 'Despite increasing popular interest in acupuncture as a treatment technique, it has not been demonstrated that acupuncture is able to promote smoking cessation.'
    'Past reviews of smoking modification research indicate that aversive techniques largely have failed to help people to quit smoking.'
    'From my review of over fifty reports, comments and critiques of the use of hypnosis to control smoking, I conclude that hypnosis produces only modest results.'
    Review and Evaluation of Smoking Cessation Methods: US and Canada (1978–1985), US Department of Health and Human Services, National Institutes of Health, Washington, DC.
    'Acupuncture and nicotine gum were effective in helping smokers to stop smoking during the first month but did not reduce the tendency to relapse after that time.'
    Helping People to Stop Smoking: Randomised comparison of groups being treated with acupuncture and nicotine gum compared with control group. *British Medical Journal* (1985) 291:1538–1539.

4 *YOUR FREEDOM TO SMOKE*

'Adam was but human — this explains it all. He
did not want the apple for the apple's sake, he
wanted it only because it was forbidden.'

Mark Twain

Iᴛ's a common myth that smokers don't have any
willpower, or not as much as other people. But willpower
isn't something that gets handed out in finite amounts:
everybody has will and the power to use it. You use your
will all the time. It's in your power to choose to do or not
do something. In fact, you cannot escape using your will
every moment of your life, even if it's your will to do
nothing.

So why is it that some people aren't able to make effective
use of their will to stop smoking cigarettes?

The answer to this is crucial to understanding the process
of stopping smoking. What you need to know about will is
that it works best when it is freely directed. All our will is
free will, and a great many smokers make the fatal mistake
of believing that they surrender their free will (their
freedom to smoke) when they stop smoking.

Thinking this way has disastrous consequences: the
misery of feeling deprived.

What You Think is What You Will Feel

The most important thing to understand about the experience of deprivation is that it is purely and simply a state of
mind – and you can change your state of mind.

Although most people will agree that stopping smoking
is something they are choosing to do, in their own private
thoughts they in fact deny their choice to smoke.

Usually when people stop smoking what they keep saying

to themselves is: 'Now I mustn't smoke!' or 'I really can't smoke any more!' These 'can't' and 'mustn't' thoughts have the effect of making them feel deprived. *Feelings of deprivation are actually feelings of anger, loss and frustration which spring from thinking you are being denied access to something you want.*

But when you think more carefully about it, no one else has, in fact, deprived you of smoking. And no one could, unless they had physically locked you up and taken away your cigarettes! Then you really *cannot* smoke. You genuinely do not have any choice about whether or not you do smoke. But that is the *only* kind of situation in which your choice has been removed.

If you were suddenly locked up without cigarettes, then your reaction would be understandable. You would feel deprived because you really would be deprived.

If, after you stop smoking, you tell yourself you *can't* smoke, your mind reacts exactly *as if* you had been locked up in a cell and all your cigarettes had been taken away.

And if you yourself don't stay in touch with your free choice to smoke or not to smoke, if instead you use prohibiting words to yourself, like saying 'I can't smoke' or 'I mustn't smoke', then you are simulating depriving yourself. And you will rebel against this just as surely as if someone tried to take your cigarettes, or your freedom, away.

The feelings we call 'deprivation' are always based on the delusion that our freedom is being denied. If you make free choices, out of your own free will, then it will be obvious that you are not being 'deprived'.

'I Have to Stop'

As important as the 'I can't' belief is the 'I have to' attitude. Even while you are smoking, you may well be thinking to yourself, 'I have to stop smoking'. Many smokers say this to themselves every day. A common train of thought is, 'If I go on smoking, my health will deteriorate. I can't let that happen. Therefore, I have to stop smoking.'

In fact, this is never really true. When you believe that

you have to stop, you fail to acknowledge that you have the choice to continue — whether you like it or not! You do, in fact, have the freedom to go on smoking *and* have your health deteriorate.

If you stop smoking believing that you have to stop, you are telling yourself you have no choice about it, that you are being forced, or forcing yourself, to stop. Stopping smoking becomes, instead of the liberation it really is, a sentence of doom.

The extent to which you believe that you have to stop is the extent to which you will experience deprivation when you do stop.

No wonder smokers keep procrastinating about stopping! Most smokers are living their lives telling themselves that they have to stop smoking — but not today.

A thought that has quite different implications is, 'I want to stop smoking.' This suggests you are making a free choice to achieve something.

However, as soon as anyone gets serious about stopping, their attitude is usually: 'I don't really want to stop, but I have to.' And they forget that stopping smoking is something that they really do *want* to do.

When you accept that you don't ever *have* to, you may begin to see that, in fact, you do really *want* to.

Symptoms of Deprivation

Almost all smokers believe themselves to be deprived, to some degree, during the process of stopping smoking, but the experience can be very different for different kinds of people.

Anger and irritability are very common. Some ex-smokers will pick fights with people, become intolerant, impatient, aggressive and even rude. It can seem that their personality has completely changed since they stopped smoking.

Others feel martyred and resentful about having stopped. All the fun has gone out of their lives. They may become profoundly depressed, withdrawn and apathetic, even to the point of thinking that a life without smoking may not be worth living.

There is often a deep sense of self-pity and it is not unusual to start envying other people who are still smoking. They think, 'Poor me, lucky them'.

When you feel deprived, you see stopping smoking as a great loss. Tears are shed, as if something wonderful had been taken away from them, *against their will*. They feel like victims. They feel trapped. It feels like there's a huge void in their life that won't ever be filled.

At this stage, your past life as a smoker can begin to look like 'the good old days'. You become obsessed with smoking, and begin to figure out ways to justify going back to it. Perhaps you start an argument with someone (especially a person who has been pushing you to stop) or you stage some kind of drama so that you have a good excuse to smoke. Or you make do with a not so good excuse.

While you have a sense of deprivation your desire to smoke won't diminish. It becomes exaggerated, more intense, and you can still be yearning for a smoke for hours at a time, months after stopping — if you can keep yourself from smoking for that long.

By far the most undermining effect of this state of deprivation is to completely lose sight of your motivation to stay stopped. Perhaps, when you were smoking, you were highly motivated to stop. You were sick of smoking, desperately wanting to get it out of your life for ever. So you stopped, but now, instead of feeling joy and relief, you feel as if you are being punished — even tortured! You don't see anything good at all about not smoking. Life without smoking looks dull, boring and intolerable. And then you really can't remember one reason why you ever thought of giving up such a fabulous pastime!

In very extreme cases, the state of deprivation creates a blind panic, a tremendous anxiety which can manifest itself in psychosomatic symptoms of fear and anxiety.

Feeling deprived makes stopping smoking dramatic and unbearable, and blows everything up out of all proportion. One person may feel a bit light-headed and disorientated when they stop smoking, but they take that in their stride. Someone experiencing extreme deprivation will over-react to that by concluding that they are losing their mind.

If you allow this sense of deprivation to persist, it's going to be virtually impossible for you to stay stopped: it's very difficult to stay motivated to keep on depriving yourself!

Difficult Circumstances

There are certain circumstances in which you are more likely to fall for the 'can't/have to' belief, and experience deprivation as a consequence. If one of the following situations applies to you, however, it doesn't mean you will be unable to stop, because if you know what is causing your feelings you can do something to change them.

□ **Serious health fears** Possibly the most common and strongest sense of deprivation is found with smokers who are deeply concerned about the state of their health. If you have become really frightened by symptoms such as heart palpitations, severe coughing or gasping for breath, you can become too frightened to even consider the possibility that you can continue to smoke. You may even have had a doctor tell you, in no uncertain terms, that you *have to* stop.

The irony is that if you don't change your thinking you are likely to end up smoking, despite your best intentions and efforts to stop. If left uncorrected, the strength of your belief that you *have* to stop creates such a powerful sense of deprivation that staying stopped becomes extremely difficult.

□ **Illness of relative or friend** If you ever have witnessed a serious illness and/or death from a smoking-related disease, you will almost certainly have formed a strong belief that you simply 'mustn't' let that happen to you.

□ **Specific health problems** You might have a particular health problem which, although not caused by smoking, will contribute to the belief that you aren't free to be a smoker. People with diabetes or asthma often feel especially pressured to stop by their condition. You might have been born with a particular weakness of the lungs or heart.

□ **Pressure from other people** If you stop smoking primarily because someone else has asked or told you to, you hold them responsible for your decision to stop, and this can create an intolerable state of deprivation.

As a smoker, you may be told incessantly that you 'have to' stop smoking, or that you 'can't smoke' in certain situations. Loved ones may threaten to leave you, or may try to strike bargains aimed at pressuring you to stop.

More and more employers are introducing restrictions on smokers. Everywhere you go, it seems that people are telling you that you 'can't smoke' any more. (Or 'must not', 'should not' or 'ought not', which give rise to the same feelings.)

□ **Obligation**   Stopping smoking because of a sense of obligation to others is another way in which people create feelings of deprivation. Parents may feel obliged to stop because of the effect of their smoking on their children, both in the sense of being bad role models and because of the dangers of passive smoking.

□ **Pregnancy**   Obviously the obligation to the unborn child can create a powerful belief that you 'have to' stop smoking. And the sense of deprivation that arises from this makes it very difficult to do. It is currently estimated that *only one in twelve* smoking mothers-to-be actually stop smoking during pregnancy. (1)

It's not that pregnant women don't have good reasons to stop smoking; they certainly do. The point is that there is a crucial difference between having good reasons to stop and thinking that you 'have to' stop.

□ **Role models and closet smokers**   You might work in a job that creates a particular kind of pressure to stop smoking. You may believe, because of your profession, that you should set a good example for others, and should not be seen to be a smoker.

You may even hide the fact that you smoke and become a closet (secret) smoker. Nicotine gum can be a way for someone to hide their smoking, but a sense of deprivation keeps the addiction fuelled. This may be particularly true among people in health professions, and the clergy.

Another kind of closet smoker hides their smoking because they are so obviously ill from it, and the tremendous guilt they feel is sure to lead to a very strong sense of deprivation when they finally stop.

□ **Strict upbringing** If you had a very disciplined child-
hood you may well attach an especially high value to any
act of rebellion, especially smoking. If you were told that
smoking is a sin, it's understandable that you regard it as
forbidden. Stopping smoking, even much later on in life,
can still be seen as a capitulation to the rule 'thou shalt not
smoke', resulting in a sense of deprivation.

'Can't, Must, Got to, Have to'

You might see all kinds of things in your life in terms of
things that you 'have to' or 'can't' do, so stopping smoking
becomes just one more thing that you approach with this
attitude.

'Can't' and 'have to' are frequently misused in everyday
thought and speech. For example, you might say: 'I can't
have dinner with you tonight'. This, of course, does not
usually mean that you're physically incapable or forbidden.
It simply means you have another engagement that you are
choosing to keep.

Often, this choice of words doesn't create much of a
problem. In fact, many people get lots of things accom-
plished by believing that they have no choice but to do
them. When it comes to stopping smoking, however, your
choice of words — and therefore the way you think —
makes the difference between failure and success because
of the intolerable problem of feeling deprived.

If you are the sort of person who says 'I have to' and 'I
can't' a lot, you will need to work to alter your way of
thinking. And, if you do this with smoking, the overall
benefit can affect many other areas of your life as well.

Take Responsibility and You Take Control

Feeling deprived also indicates that you are not taking full
responsibility for yourself and your own actions. If you
really are locked up without cigarettes, the cell is responsible for the fact that you are not smoking – not you.

It's an error we are all susceptible to because in each of
us there remains the little child we once were, the record

in our memories of a time when we really *weren't* responsible for ourselves. When you stop smoking by telling yourself: 'You are not allowed to smoke!', the child in you becomes actively rebellious.

Becoming psychologically responsible is something we all do by degrees. It is the process of coming to recognise that you are the creator of what you think, feel and do. And it is you and you alone who determines whether you smoke or not!

You might be the kind of person who has difficulty in doing that because you have a strong tendency to blame others, refusing to see your own part in any of the situations in your life. Whether you are smoking or stopping smoking, you see it as just one more thing that makes you a victim of circumstance.

When you stop smoking, you subconsciously blame others and project your anger on to the people around you — family, friends or complete strangers.

Some end up believing they are really very angry people and that smoking is the only thing that keeps their anger under wraps. It certainly can seem that way if you don't understand what's really going on in your mind.

If this seems to apply to you, it doesn't mean that you won't be able to stop smoking. Just remember that stopping smoking is *your choice*, and that nobody else has done this to you. You may feel angry and resentful when you stop, but it's because you have forgotten about your freedom of choice: all you need to do is remind yourself.

If you are attempting to stop smoking purely because of someone else, my advice to you is: *don't*.

Sacrifice and Reward

When you tell yourself you *can't* smoke, smoking becomes forbidden fruit and, as everybody knows, that's always the sweetest. In order to compensate for this sense of sacrifice, you will feel a great need to reward yourself. The rewards can take the form of buying extravagant presents for yourself or eating extra, especially 'forbidden' food, such as chocolate.

You can also think that you ought to be rewarded in some way by your family and friends and can get very upset with them for not being especially nice to you when you've stopped smoking. This is particularly likely if you have stopped smoking to please them.

If you approach stopping as a choice rather than as a deprivation, you will be able to see that not smoking is its own reward. Your health will improve and you will feel proud of yourself and more in control of your life. And if being an ex-smoker isn't a preferable, more rewarding way of life for you, then you can always go back to being a smoker. If you choose that it may, of course, cost you your health, and it's very likely that you will increasingly regret your dependence on smoking. But either way, it is simply your choice about how you want to live your life. Living your life as a smoker has its consequences. But *smoking is not forbidden!* You are allowed to be a smoker, if that is your wish. You always have permission.

If you have stopped smoking in the past and you felt deprived, then, when you did finally smoke, it probably seemed like a rewarding thing to do. You may have experienced a mixture of feelings: disappointment at your failure, but also a great sense of release. This is because smoking a cigarette seems to release you from the imaginary cell of your deprivation. In as much as it relieves the symptoms of the 'deprivation', it will cheer you up, calm you down, please and reward you. This is why it's so important to overcome your beliefs about having been deprived. If you don't, you will end up reinforcing your addiction.

Rebellion

If it seems to you that stopping smoking has made you feel locked up, smoking a cigarette becomes your key to freedom.

Many smokers start smoking in order to prove that they are free to smoke. A great many continue to smoke and then find themselves stuck with smoking, unable to stop even for the briefest time, in order to maintain a sense of freedom. It's a crazy trap.

You can tell when 'rebellious' smokers are anticipating feeling deprived because they increase the amount they are smoking whenever they get serious about stopping, or, for example, are told to stop by a doctor. About a third of smokers in my classes smoke more than usual just before they begin the course. They are making sure that they don't feel trapped and deprived even before they stop smoking! These are the people who believe that they 'have to' stop, and are already rebelling against that restriction.

Many smokers make attempts to stop smoking, only to feel deprived because of the imagined loss of freedom, and then go back to smoking in order to prove, once again, that they are free to smoke: 'Nobody can tell me what to do! I can smoke and I will! I'll show them!'

A rebellion implies that a restriction of some kind has been imposed. *You cannot rebel if you already have complete freedom.*

You Need to Feel Free

The truth is that you are free to be a smoker. There will be consequences for you should you take that path. But these consequences, however terrifying, do not take away your freedom to smoke. They are the consequences you get if you exercise that freedom by smoking.

This is your life, and you are free to live it as a smoker if that is your choice. You can smoke. You can go on smoking. You can smoke even more each day than you do now. You can smoke every day of your life and never stop.

I'm not encouraging you to do that: living your life as a smoker will cost you dearly. It will cost you your health, money and your self-esteem. It may also cost you jobs, relationships and perhaps even your life. What I'm encouraging you to do is to find a way to stop smoking without developing a sense of deprivation, so that you will be able to stay stopped. And the way to do that is to understand — *and really believe* — that stopping smoking doesn't limit your freedom to smoke, in any way.

The most important thing to know about stopping

smoking is: *you don't have to do it.* Ever!

Does this sound like a dangerous way of thinking? It's very possible that you are afraid to tell yourself you are free to be a smoker.

The fear, of course, is that if you give yourself that option to smoke, you will actually take it. So you try to eliminate it by convincing yourself that you have no choice but to stop. And that's exactly how you create the misery of feeling deprived.

Overcoming Deprivation

If you are reading this as a smoker, the fact that you can smoke may seem rather obvious. Here you are, lighting up cigarettes and smoking them. Of course you can do that. It's after you have made an attempt to stop that your choice to go back to smoking can seem to have been surrendered.

The work involved in stopping smoking is in coming to understand that you have the freedom to be a smoker — even though you are not exercising that freedom by smoking.

This mental adjustment may sound relatively easy, but the chances are that you have a deep-seated belief that you have been developing for many years, even decades. And it takes some time and effort to turn this false way of thinking around.

A recent client of mine, Susan, is typical of someone working through a substantial problem with deprivation. When she first stopped smoking she got angry, then lethargic. When I spoke to her a week later she was feeling very deprived, yearning to smoke for hours on end, even though she was genuinely horrified by the thought of going back to smoking. Understandably, she said that she didn't feel very confident at all. She told me that she couldn't smoke. Her (false) logic was that if she wanted to stay off smoking, then she didn't have the option of smoking. 'If I want to live', she said, 'then I can't smoke.' 'Not true,' I told her. 'You want to live; true. Smoking will kill you; quite possible. But the truth is that you still have the option of doing that. It's a freedom you have, whether you want it or not. It's a fact of life.'

I wasn't encouraging her to smoke, I was encouraging her to acknowledge that the choice to smoke exists, so that she wouldn't think she was being deprived. When she turned this thinking around she felt much more positive and in control, and found staying stopped much easier.

Her background explains the trouble she was having coming to terms with the concept of free choice. Her parents were both heavy smokers. While they smoked and smoked every day, they always told her, over and over again, that she 'must never become a smoker'. They were both very ill from smoking, and understandably wanted a better life for their daughter. Susan started smoking when she was sixteen and you can imagine the reaction when her parents found out. There was much screaming and yelling and again she was told that she was not allowed to smoke, that she '*had* to stop'.

Once, a few years ago, she stopped smoking after a visit to a hypnotist, but she had just repressed her desire, and was back smoking after two weeks. She didn't even see the issue of choice and deprivation until she came to my course, after thirty years of smoking, simultaneously believing that she wasn't allowed to smoke.

When she reminds herself that she does, in fact, *have the freedom to smoke*, not smoking becomes easier and more positive. Her desire to smoke is significantly more tolerable, when before it was 'like a scream through my body'. Knowing that she has a choice provided the key.

She will probably go through periods of forgetting her freedom, but then she will remember it again, eventually shifting her thinking enough so that her choices are real to her.

Sometimes it does take a while for the penny to drop, and this is what causes the initial difficulty in stopping smoking. So it's important to keep on reminding yourself that you are *free* to be a smoker. You may understand that you have the choice to smoke, but only on a relatively superficial level. You see the logic, but inside you are still rebelling against the belief that you are not really free. It takes a while for your thinking to change on every level.

Many people feel the effects of thinking they are deprived,

but are not aware of the thinking that is causing them. In fact, most people aren't even aware that it is thinking that is causing it at all. Often a client who has been feeling deprived for a week or two will say to me, 'When will it get better?' 'When you change the way you are thinking,' I reply. A common mistake is to believe that the sense of deprivation is caused by something physical, like a flu virus, and must be patiently tolerated until it runs its course. I have seen the transformation in so many people, though, who have made that all-important shift in their thinking and *instantly stopped feeling deprived!*

□ *If you feel angry*, remind yourself that nobody is making you do this and that you have not trapped yourself: you are free to smoke — it's up to you.

□ *If you feel grief*, remember that you have not lost anything; smoking is completely available to you.

□ *If you forget your motivation*, remember that you are not locked into one irrevocable decision: you can go back to smoking. Consider that option carefully and honestly, and if you have any motivation at all to stay stopped, it will become obvious.

Stopping smoking doesn't have to feel like a restriction and a tragedy: it can be a liberation and a genuine reward. But you will only experience it that way while you really understand you have still got the choice to return to smoking.

That choice doesn't exist only at the time you stop: a return to smoking continues to be an alternative for the rest of your life, and this can be difficult to accept, especially if you have a strong fear of failure. How to enjoy your freedom to smoke — and not deny it or fear it — is what we will be looking at next.

In other words   RUTH

*I began smoking when I was about eight, but did not
take it up seriously until I was fourteen or fifteen. My
intake rose steadily until in my early forties I was
smoking around eighty cigarettes a day. If I happened to
stay up late, as I quite often did, I could go up to one
hundred and twenty.*

*I tried to stop on a number of occasions. My main
reason for wanting to stop was self-disgust at my utter
dependence and the fact that they really had come to
dominate my life. I fretted about not being able to
smoke on the tube or in the houses of those who
objected.*

*What was most helpful in the Full Stop course was the
removal of that sense of mental deprivation that
essentially wrecked every previous attempt of mine to
stop smoking. The training of my subconscious to grasp
that I wasn't being prevented from smoking, but was
utterly free to do so at any time, was what made a
crucial difference.*

*The best thing about not smoking is the sense of
freedom. I encourage friends of mine to give up according
to this method, but I don't nag. One of the other great
virtues of the course was that it didn't turn me into one
of those awful converts who go around condemning
smokers. I am untroubled by having smokers around me.
My house is full of ashtrays, I don't mind the smell even
of stale smoke, and active smoke I quite enjoy.*

References

1. UK Department of Health statistic. *British Medical Journal* (1991)
    302:552.

5 CHOOSING FOR NOW

'. . . he explained that I was really suffering from
my resolutions much more than from the
cigarettes. I ought to try and cure myself
without making any resolutions.'

Italo Svevo, *Confessions of Zeno*

M ANY people who have attended my course tell me,
much later on, that they never expected to stop
smoking and stay stopped. The chances are they had tried
to stop many times before, both on their own and with other
kinds of help, and had failed over and over again. It's probable
that you also, to a greater or lesser extent, have a conviction
that even if you stop, you will not be able to stay stopped for
very long. It's a common and understandable concern to have.
The problem, however, is not with your expectation of
failure, but with the way you try to cope with it.

To begin with, you may cope with it by not making any
attempt at all to stop smoking: if you don't try, you won't
fail! You may tell yourself you are waiting until you are
more motivated, because then, you think, you will be more
likely to succeed. However, the motivation you are probably waiting for is a serious threat to your health: most
smokers justify their smoking by reasoning that if anything
serious really did happen, then of course they would stop.

*But bad health doesn't remove your concerns about
failure, it increases them.* I have talked to many smokers
who find themselves stuck between the devil and the deep
blue sea: fearing not making any attempt to stop because
smoking is causing serious illness, and fearing making an
attempt that fails.

Sooner or later, though, your fears push you into trying
to stop. You make a solemn commitment to never smoke
again. You reason that in order to stop smoking and
successfully stay stopped, you must make a commitment

which, once made, you are bound to keep. It's a final decision, made once and for all, and the possibility of smoking again is not to be considered.

The Commitment Trap

The irony is that it is precisely this way of thinking that keeps so many smokers from even attempting to stop. Or, even if they do, it is absolutely bound to make them feel such deprivation that it becomes impossible to keep to their commitment! *Making a commitment never to smoke again is equivalent to denying your freedom to smoke.* As you know from the last chapter, you need to stay in touch with your freedom to smoke so that you don't feel deprived. The problem, however, is that for many people who stop smoking the possibility of failure is so awful they don't want to admit it exists at all.

Of course, if you really could eliminate your freedom to smoke, you would indeed be secure. If you really were locked up for ever in a cell with no cigarettes, you would definitely be successful at stopping smoking! But, assuming that you do have access to them, this sense of security is a dangerous illusion.

This explains why it is that some smokers can appear to be so very motivated to stop, yet fail over and over again. The more desperate they are to stop smoking, the more they throw themselves into the cell of a total commitment to stop for ever, and the more trapped and deprived they end up feeling. So, after a brief and agonising period of time, they break down and smoke, only to feel even more desperate the next time they try to stop. It's a vicious circle! And, unless you are aware of the attitude you are taking, you may create this very situation for yourself.

As with all the difficulties that smokers create in their attempts to stop, there is a simple way to change your thinking so it becomes positive and realistic. If you really want to stay stopped this time, you need to overcome your fear of failure without denying your freedom to fail. And the way to do that is to choose to stop smoking *only for the present time.*

Now, Now, and Now . . .

If you make a choice to stop smoking, how long does that choice last? You might want it to last for at least an hour. You might want it to last for ever. But life doesn't work that way.

The reality is that you can only make a choice as to whether you smoke or not when you actually make it, right in that moment, in the here and now. For example, if you make a choice to stop smoking at 12.30, then even before 12.31, you have a whole new choice to make. As the existence of choice always implies alternatives, you *could* make a choice to smoke at 12.31! Or, you *could* make another choice *not* to smoke.

When you stop smoking, you don't start out by making a commitment to never smoke again. You start out by making a choice not to smoke only for that moment. And you bear in mind that you will be making many more choices as you go along.

At first, this may sound unbearable, even impossible. It seems a lot easier to make one resolution and convince yourself that you *have* to stick to it. But remember that, in fact, this is a much more difficult route. Once you have truly accepted this principle, making choices only for the present time will become simple and obvious. Remember also that the desire to smoke, and therefore the process of making choices, becomes much less frequent as time goes on.

When you stop smoking by declaring 'I've smoked my last cigarette — I'll never smoke again!' you deny your freedom to smoke, and put yourself straight into the cell of deprivation. Even if you only predict that you won't smoke for the next hour, then for that hour you are going to feel deprived.

By all means, set a *goal* of staying stopped. But as you do this, remember that you can only reach that goal by making real choices in the here and now. *There is always the choice to go back to smoking.* Knowing this makes the difference between feeling deprived or feeling free, and therefore genuinely able to choose.

Loss and Grief

Smokers often describe their experience of stopping as a process of grieving. They see their cigarettes as companions with whom they had a kind of relationship for a major part of their lives. When smokers 'give up' this relationship, they often say they are mourning a great loss, the passing on of these 'friends'.

There are, however, crucial distinctions. First of all, cigarettes aren't your friends, any more than a bottle of booze is a friend to an alcoholic or a syringe to a heroin addict. This is nothing but a delusion of drug addiction.

Even more significant, though, is that *you don't lose your cigarettes when you stop smoking.* The sense of loss comes from the assumption that you will never smoke again. When someone dies, they are gone forever. That's why you grieve: you will never see them again. It's final and it's out of your control.

When you stop smoking only for the present time, you keep in sight the fact that you could return to smoking at any point. There is always a possibility that you could go back to smoking and perhaps end up smoking every day for the rest of your life.

If you really take that fact in, there is no need to grieve. You will be aware, of course, that you are not smoking, but there is a big difference between noticing that you've stopped and feeling as if you've lost something.

At first, staying stopped can be a bit of a balancing act, like walking along the edge of a cliff, knowing that you could make one false move and end it all. Instead of pretending that the cliff doesn't exist, what works is to master walking along this edge.

Pressure from Others

During the first couple of weeks after you have stopped, it is especially helpful to remember about choosing for now when you talk to others about your smoking. If you have taken my advice and kept the whole thing quiet, it might be a while before they catch on to what you are doing. As you can probably now see, the longer you keep quiet about having stopped, the better.

Sooner or later, though, someone will notice that you haven't been smoking and they might ask you directly if you've stopped. It's going to be best for you to say something that doesn't make you feel as though you've made a permanent commitment. Say something like: 'Well, I'm cutting down, I don't know if I'll stop', or 'I might have one later'. It doesn't matter what *they* think. What matters is that you have kept in touch with your choices. So far, so good. You haven't locked yourself into any irrevocable decision.

If you go around telling everybody you've stopped smoking, you create a stronger sense of being trapped into staying stopped, which is disastrous for your motivation. Their pressure on you to stay stopped will act to enhance your sense of deprivation, and that's the very last thing you need. Other people can put the pressure on in the most innocent ways, even by saying things like: 'Good for you!' or, 'Keep it up!' If you are feeling deprived, you'll probably want to hit them. It's also likely that you'll find yourself close to lighting up a cigarette. It's just as if they are telling you that you can't ever smoke again, so all you want to do is rebel.

Margaret, a woman in her fifties who had smoked for over forty years, told me about a conversation she had with her father a few weeks after she had attended a Full Stop course. Her father took her hand and, with tears in his eyes, he thanked her sincerely for having stopped smoking, saying that he was immensely proud of what she had done.

Margaret told me that although she knew he was expressing his love for her, and that his acknowledgement was very much appreciated, she felt a surge of rebellion well up inside her as he spoke. She thanked him for his concern, and privately she reminded herself that she was still free to go back to smoking. She continues to make free choices not to smoke, just for now, based on what she wants for herself.

Other clients have had similar reactions, feeling obliged to another to stay stopped as a result of gifts — a piece of jewellery or a bunch of flowers — given as a reward for stopping.

I'll Worry About it When I Get There

There's another kind of problem that comes from fear about the future. It's common when you first stop smoking to get worried about particular activities or events, wondering if you will actually be able to handle them without smoking.

You might be anxious about a party or a special work project. It might be meeting that special friend with whom you used to chain smoke and talk for hours. Or it might be a familiar activity, like talking on the phone or driving long distances, where you have developed an especially strong connection with smoking. Whatever it is, you can bet there will be something, sooner or later, after you have stopped, that you will become concerned about.

You might try to project yourself into the future and imagine yourself doing these things without smoking. This will not be very helpful. It's quite possible that your mind does not have a picture of you doing these things without smoking, so it cannot deal with them at all. You have no experience, no memory to refer to.

So, you create a tremendous amount of anxiety because you are sure you will never make it through this situation without smoking. Since you can't imagine it, having never done it, the anxiety keeps building up. If you don't overcome your anxiety, the next step is for you to smoke because you are sure that you will have to do that at some point anyway.

But it's not the situation that causes you to smoke — it's your anxiety about the situation. It's your *fear* of failure that leads you to fail.

I'm not going to suggest that you should never think about the future, because that's impossible. It would be ridiculous to pretend that you will never think at all about certain situations, and whether or not you'll smoke.

But if you start to *worry* and get anxious about them, simply remind yourself that you can only choose whether or not you smoke in present time. You have no way of knowing how you will handle a situation in the future. You can never know whether or not you will smoke at the party on Saturday night until you are there, making your choices.

The key to success is being willing to not know for sure. Of course, it would be comforting to have some kind of guarantee that you won't fail, but the fact is, there is always a risk, and that's just the way life is. You might smoke and you might not. All you can ever do is choose for now not to smoke and hope that you continue to do that.

It can be helpful to anticipate that you will have a strong desire to smoke when you are in a particular situation: just remember that you can only deal with that desire *at the time you are experiencing it.*

You can only be in control of your smoking in the present time. So when you stop trying to predict the future and bring yourself back into the here and now, you put yourself in control.

So Far, So Good

If you have been smoking, daily, for many years, not smoking will quite possibly feel strange at first, even unnatural. It's unlikely that you will feel confident as soon as you've stopped, but the longer you stay off and the more situations you handle without smoking, the more confident you will become. Confidence is something you acquire, gradually.

The techniques described in Part Two of this book are very effective. The more effort you put into working with them, the more confident you will become that, not only do they work, but you are capable of using them. You learn to trust yourself that you will continue to use them, no matter what is going on in your life. This is something you can only find out for yourself as you go along: it's difficult to be sure of it ahead of time.

Many smokers make the mistake of putting off stopping smoking because they are waiting to feel confident. They want to wait until they are sure they will succeed before making an attempt to stop. They might be waiting for a very long time.

Don't wait for your fear of failure to go away. Stopping smoking will always be somewhat frightening, because you never know how it will turn out.

It's much, much less frightening if you just do it moment by moment. So far, so good, and wait and see what happens.

One client, Richard, says that he doesn't even call himself an ex-smoker because it sounds too final. He says that he is a smoker who just isn't smoking right now. He's been saying that for well over a year, so far.

Choosing for now keeps you in reality. But what happens if, after perhaps a whole year of making choices not to smoke, you then make a choice to smoke? If you have the freedom to smoke, shouldn't you exercise it at least once in a while? This is the subject of our next chapter.

In other words   *DEE*

I don't think I ever believed I would stop smoking. I had been a smoker for twenty-six years. I smoked twenty to thirty a day — or forty if life was more exciting, conversation was intense, or during panic situations. I loved my cigarette breaks and the social side that accompanied them.

The course gave me the tools to fight my battle: staying in the present time helped stop panic about even the next ten minutes. I worked hard at stopping smoking, and every time I talked myself through a desire to smoke and gave myself the choices, I felt stronger, more proud of myself and totally surprised that I was doing it. I still am. I still have the original cigarettes in my desk with access to more if I want, but I have not had so much as one puff since I stopped two and a half years ago. And, because I don't feel that I am depriving myself of anything, I have not joined the angry mob of ex-smokers.

I was amazed to find myself having a desire to smoke recently: I went through my 'talk' and made my choice to accept the desire. I feel I have been empowered by the course and that I have given myself a huge gift by stopping smoking.

---

6 ONE MORE PUFF

'The dance of the last cigarette which began
when I was twenty has not yet reached its
last figure yet . . . I may as well say that for
some time past I have been smoking a great
many cigarettes and have given up calling
them the last.'

Italo Svevo, *Confessions of Zeno*

SMOKING is not just a bad habit, it's a drug addiction. I'm
not saying this to make you feel guilty, but to help you
deal with the facts.

As Chapter Two explains, the addiction is much more a
product of the mind than of the body. But it is none the less
real and problematic. It's a collection of powerful lies, or
delusions, and taking control of your smoking is the process
of identifying those lies and discovering the truth.

Frequently, people in the process of stopping smoking say
that there are two opposing voices, like two completely
different people inside their head, arguing. Of course, you
are only one, whole person: the other voice is that of the
addiction that you have added on to yourself over the years.
Some people say it's the Devil talking. This argument is
part of the process of stopping smoking, and this book
provides you with every bit of information you need to
work through the argument and resolve the mental conflict.

Think of it as a game. Any time you stop smoking, the
game is that the addiction tries to figure out how to get you
to go back to smoking. It will be marvellously creative and
have you convinced of the most ridiculous things. You will
be able to see through some of the deceptions very clearly,
and even laugh at them. Others will be more difficult.

The most compelling and persistent of all the deceptions
is the idea that, at some point, you will be able to smoke
one or two cigarettes without returning to an uncontroll-

able, daily dependency. If you believe this to be true, it's probably the most convincing excuse to smoke that there is. After all, one cigarette isn't going to kill you: it's 'simply not a problem'.

Of course, there are a few — just a very few — people who only smoke occasionally, which is what makes you think it is possible. But the odds are against you.

So many people go back to smoking as a direct result of this mistake. Some people even make this mistake over and over again, never learning from their past experience! It looks like such a great solution, the smoker's dream of only smoking sometimes: just at parties, or just for a day or two to help you through something difficult.

The 'something difficult' can even be withdrawal itself, which is the craziest justification of them all. Yes, smoking will certainly help ease your withdrawal symptoms, but then you will be smoking again.

When your addiction has convinced you that just one more cigarette is all you will ever want again, then you are being seriously conned.

All or Nothing

First of all, look at your own experience of smoking by estimating the total number of cigarettes you have ever smoked. You may not want to do this, but it's very powerful information. If you have smoked twenty a day for only a year, then you have already smoked about 7,300 cigarettes. If you've been at it for ten years, you've smoked 73,000. Thirty a day for ten years is almost 110,000 cigarettes.

Do you really believe that one cigarette is all you will ever want? You do tend to smoke them one at a time, but each one is just a part of a way of life.

When you smoke, you integrate smoking into your life and you live the life of a smoker. You smoke day in, day out, year in, year out, no matter what. You smoke when you are happy and when you are sad. You smoke when you are busy and when you are bored. You smoke when you are hungry and when you are full. You smoke when you are under stress and when you are relaxing.

Of course, different people smoke different amounts; one person may smoke twenty a day and another sixty. You know what kind of a smoker you are, and how much you usually smoke. That amount, whatever it is for you, is what you will be choosing to return to any time you choose to smoke. The cigarette that is just one more is really the first of thousands more.

According to the *British Journal of Addiction* (1990): 'Over ninety per cent of teenagers who smoke three to four cigarettes are trapped into a career of regular smoking which typically lasts for some thirty to forty years.' If three or four cigarettes got you hooked in the first place, what are the chances of smoking just a few once the addiction is already established in your mind?

The truth is that you are an addicted smoker and addiction means being out of control. It is simply impossible for nicotine to become not addictive for you.

Resenting yourself for having become an addicted smoker won't help you at all. It is much better to admit that you did it, without blame. In fact, the more you forgive yourself for having started smoking, the more likely it is that you will stop and stay stopped. Just like millions of other people, you got conned by the same lies. It doesn't mean you are bad or stupid.

This is one thing that makes smoking so different from most other drug addictions: the most stable and well-adjusted people can become totally hooked. The mistake is to refuse to believe that you have become addicted to what is arguably the most powerful addiction of them all.

I've Slipped a Bit

Eventually most smokers reluctantly come to admit that they are incapable of smoking in a controlled way. They know from their own experience that when they smoke, it's all day, every day. But another deception that smokers live with is that this way of life won't continue for long.

It's very likely that when you started smoking, you didn't think that you would continue to smoke for as long as you have. You probably didn't think much about it at all, or if you did, you just thought that you'd stop some time soon — not now, of course, but before too long. I don't think that many smokers start out by intending to go on smoking every day for the rest of their lives.

There is a common myth that the more times you try to stop smoking, the more likely it is that you will succeed. Repeated failures could be part of a learning process, but they can also lead to a profound sense of hopelessness about ever being able to stay stopped for good.

If you think success *next* time will be that much more likely, remember that *you also run the risk of never stopping again*. It's a possibility that very few smokers want to acknowledge. You might stop again — but what if you don't?

You don't have to learn everything the hard way. You don't have to get run over by a car in order to learn how to stop and look before you cross a road.

When you have stopped smoking and are considering the question of smoking again, consider this: if I choose to smoke, I will return to smoking and it's *possible* that I will continue to smoke every day for the rest of my life.

Is There Really a Choice?

Many people think that not being able to smoke the odd cigarette is in direct contradiction to having the freedom to smoke. Admitting that smoking one cigarette, even just lighting one up, will re-ignite the addiction leads many ex-smokers to conclude that they 'can't smoke ever again'.

So, once more, the ex-smoker creates major feelings of deprivation. And, once more, they are all caused by errors in thinking. *The choice to smoke is an all-or-nothing choice, but it's still a choice*. It's a choice to return to addictive, compulsive behaviour and run the risk of never being able to control it again. But it's still a real alternative, and a freedom that you have.

The only choice you do not have is to smoke in a controlled, non-addictive way.

If you don't stay in touch with your freedom to smoke, then you might be tempted to prove that you're really free by actually going ahead and doing it. 'I'll just have one,' or

'I'll just smoke for a bit and stop again later,' is the easy way out; your way of justifying smoking.

Often it is something that is done on the spur of the moment, 'without really thinking'. Many people say that if they had stopped and thought about it for a moment, then of course they would not have smoked.

That is precisely why it is so important to acknowledge the significance of lighting up a cigarette again, after you have stopped. As one of my clients explained: 'There are micro-seconds between thought and ignition, and it's only by forcing yourself into that gap that you can stop yourself from smoking.'

If, in the back of your mind, you still think that smoking a bit is a problem you can handle later, then lighting up will be an easy option for you, especially when you've got some kind of crisis as an excuse.

It's like the difference between holding a toy gun in your hands, or picking up one that is real, and loaded. Cigarettes are like a real, loaded gun, and it is both helpful and appropriate to treat them with the same degree of respect for the power that they possess.

How, then, should you handle the problem of 'passive smoking'? If you find yourself in a very smoky environment, you can inhale the equivalent of a couple of cigarettes and have nicotine in your blood stream. But this does not mean you will go back to smoking, as long as you have not made a choice to smoke. You may or may not experience a desire to smoke in the company of smokers, but this has no connection with passive smoking.

Once again, it's not the presence or absence of nicotine in your body, but what is going on in your mind, that causes you to smoke. It's your mind, not your body chemistry, that will get you back smoking once you have lit a cigarette, even if you don't inhale it.

I'll Smoke One Now and Choose Not to Later

It can seem so logical: since choices last only for the moment, then after you smoke one, with your next choice you can decide not to smoke again. The trouble with this deception is that your choices aren't *equal*. You are addicted to smoking, and never become addicted to not smoking. *Your choice to smoke is your choice to return to a drug addiction.*

Once you have smoked one cigarette, or even just part of one, you may have a number of different reactions. First of all, you might enjoy it and you might not. That really doesn't make any difference: you are just as likely to relapse if you hated your first puff.

The most common reactions are either to decide that you have failed completely and immediately go back to regular smoking, or become confident that you got away with it, and do it again.

The fewer you smoke, the more significant each one becomes. Why get serious about stopping again when you're only smoking one or two a week? Or even one or two a day? Or five a day?

Your return to smoking can be very gradual, even taking months, but you are at the thin end of the full-time smoking wedge. During this period, it seems that you have found a way to smoke non-addictively, in a controlled way. The longer you can keep it up, the more convincing it looks. But all that time you've kept your addiction fuelled — burning on the back of the stove — until finally it creeps back up to your usual level of daily smoking.

This deception is even more believable because of other people you probably know who do seem to keep smoking under control. The chances are that you know at least one person who smokes only sometimes, and this can seem to invalidate all the arguments about how addictive smoking is. How is it that some people can control how much they smoke, only smoking one or two at parties, for example?

There are a number of explanations. One is that they are not being completely truthful. It is actually very common to lie to both oneself and others about any addiction. Most smokers feel guilty about smoking and their automatic defence is, 'Well, I'm not really a smoker, you know, I just have an occasional puff or two.' I frequently have people in my classes who tell me that they hide the fact that they smoke or how much they smoke.

Another possibility is that the occasional smoker is simply a relapsed ex-smoker on his way back, slowly, to regular smoking. They say that they only smoke one or two a day, and at that time it is true. But run into them a few months later and you meet a twenty-a-day relapsed smoker. For most smokers it takes enormous effort to keep smoking under control, and they won't be able to keep it up for very long.

There are people, however, who really can control their smoking. There is a small minority of people who smoke, but simply don't ever get addicted. They really do just smoke one at Christmas. You could be one of those people, but the chances are that you are not. Otherwise, what started you on this book?

We can only guess at why those few don't get hooked. One thing to be sure of is that, for one reason or another, they don't develop a belief about deprivation. Whether they smoke or not is not a big issue: it just doesn't matter all that much. Be assured that once it has become an issue, it will continue to be one. For the vast majority of smokers, smoking is simply not a take-it-or-leave-it kind of thing.

Good Excuses

Does it make any difference if you've got a good excuse to just take one puff? In other areas of your life, it can make all the difference. If you miss a date with a friend or an important business meeting a genuine excuse can make the difference as to whether or not you lose the friend or the job.

Unfortunately, your addiction isn't your friend, and it certainly isn't something you can reason with. You might have the best excuse in the world, and nobody, including yourself, would blame you if you smoked. But you will still be smoking. You will have whatever problem it was that provided you with the good excuse — and you'll be back smoking, too.

Over the years, I have seen hundreds of people stop smoking: some stay stopped and some don't. Those who go back often have a good excuse, but those who don't have always got one or two as well. They usually say, 'Well, smoking wouldn't have helped me'. And they are right.

One lady had her handbag stolen a few weeks after stopping: and she smoked. Another had a miscarriage soon after she stopped: but she didn't smoke. One man had a close friend die in an accident a couple of months after he stopped: he didn't smoke.

Smoking just a few seems such a wonderful compromise. One thing that will help you, especially at difficult times, is to remember what the stakes really are. You either choose to smoke all the cigarettes you would end up smoking year after year, or you choose, just for now, to smoke none of them.

Your choice to light a cigarette is your choice to live your life as a smoker. After you stop, examine that option carefully and remember that it's still an option you have, and always will have. You can go back to being a smoker, any time. All you need to do is light up one cigarette.

In other words   *GILLIAN*

I smoked my first cigarette when I was seventeen. It made me feel dreadfully ill and I recall with dismay how hard I had to work at becoming an addictive smoker — and all in aid of being 'one of the group'. I persisted, and within six months I was on twenty a day.

Nineteen years and about 140,000 cigarettes later, I decided to quit, and I didn't smoke again for over two years. Cigarettes belonged to the past, I felt wonderfully well and in charge of my life. Then, at a party, someone offered me a Gauloise and I decided to have just one madly continental puff. Within six weeks I was back to twenty a day.

Twenty years and around 220,000 cigarettes later, I had a bad bout of bronchitis and a premonition of dying like this within a year. Instead, I did Full Stop.

If only I had known, twenty years earlier, the few simple techniques that are the key to the Full Stop method I would never have risked that one puff.

---

7 *WHY SMOKING SEEMS TO HELP*

'I wonder if we could contrive ... some
magnificent myth that would in itself
carry conviction to our whole community.'

Plato, *The Republic*

A T any time after you have stopped smoking, if you then
choose to smoke, you choose to be a smoker again.
Only when you take this fact into consideration do you gain
the conviction it takes not to smoke that first one. But even
though you are completely convinced that smoking one
means smoking them all, there are other deceptions the
addiction creates that can make it difficult not to take that
first puff. These deceptions are the beliefs about smoking
being helpful in various ways. We looked at this briefly in
Chapter Two.

For example, you may imagine that nicotine contributes
to your ability to do certain things, such as concentrate,
make decisions or be creative; in other words, it helps you
think. Or you may believe that it helps you to cope with
powerful emotions that you otherwise would not be able to
handle. In other words, smoking keeps you from hitting
your kids or from swearing at your boss.

Some people see cigarettes as their friends, perhaps the
only consistent element in what seems to be an unreliable
world. Others think that smoking gives them confidence or
makes them socially more assured.

This is your psychological dependency. You believe that
you are dependent on cigarettes, or nicotine, in order to live
your life the way you do.

Stopping smoking is the process of breaking free from this
dependency, and this means challenging the belief system
you have developed which says that you need to smoke.

Just because you believe something, doesn't make it true.
It is essential to acknowledge this first of all, in order to

begin to see through these delusions.

To prove this point, look at this example. Many people, including the ship's captain, believed that the *Titanic* couldn't sink. Their conviction, however, didn't make it so: they held a false belief about it. Their belief was based on what seemed to them like sound evidence: the ship was said to have been constructed so as to be unsinkable.

In the same way, you probably have what seems to you to be good reasons for your erroneous beliefs, and you also jump to false conclusions. You are, in fact, attributing capabilities to nicotine that are enormously greater than its actual chemical effect. These are delusions that any addict will create to justify his addiction.

It's usually easier to see how false these delusions are when you look from the outside into another person's dependency. The alcoholic believes that drink is making him more effective at work, but eventually he gets fired because of it. The woman who binges believes that by eating she can cheer herself up, but actually she is constantly miserable about how much she eats. The heroin addict gets a shot of self-esteem in the arm, but really the addiction leaves him feeling less than human.

In the same way, people who have never smoked look at you and puzzle about what smoking contributes to your life. You, on the other hand, are inside the dependency looking out, where it all looks completely convincing. That's the whole problem: *you believe your delusions.*

How the Delusions Are Created

You develop your beliefs about smoking along with developing the addiction. They are part of the same process: the addictive desire is interwoven with your justification for satisfying it, reinforced over and over again. Like any other belief, if you tell yourself something over and over again for years and years, you will end up very convinced. And the more you feel deprived of smoking when you stop, the more convinced you will become.

Just as it took time for you to develop the delusion, so it takes time to work through it and break it down.

Let's take one example, to see how this happens. Look at the process of writing, whether it is writing letters, a report or a story. A smoker with this delusion believes that smoking helps them to write, usually to the point where they are incapable of writing without it. So what is going on?

At some time, probably very early on in the addiction, you smoked a cigarette while writing. It only has to happen once to set up the conditioned reflex: after you have connected the activities of writing and smoking once, then the association has been established. The next time you want to write something, you have a memory of smoking while writing. This triggers a desire to smoke. You respond to your desire by smoking, and this reinforces the connection once again.

Then, whenever you get to the end of a sentence and you aren't sure of what to write next, there's a desire to smoke. This gets satisfied and reinforced before the next sentence gets written. The illusion that gets built up is that smoking helps you think of the next sentence. But in fact, all smoking does is temporarily satisfy your addictive desire to smoke.

Now, when you get around to stopping smoking, what happens is that the desire to smoke at the end of the sentence doesn't get satisfied. You will probably try to ignore it at first, perhaps by substituting mints or coffee, for example, to keep the desire at bay. But this doesn't work because mints and coffee don't satisfy a desire to smoke, and the desire becomes more and more of a problem. Concentration is completely lost as your focus is shifted from whatever you are writing to resisting the desire. So, finally, you return to smoking so that your concentration can be kept on the writing. And the belief that smoking is helping you to write is reinforced once again.

So what can you do about it? Wait until you never again need to write anything before you stop smoking? No, that won't work either because you will have different delusions about how smoking helps, depending on what you are doing. Even if you are sitting around all day with nothing to do, you can become convinced, through exactly the same process, that smoking keeps you from feeling bored. You can always invent some justification for smoking.

What helps is to see that the justifications are false, whatever they are. And the only way to do that is to tackle them head on and question them as part of the process of stopping smoking. The techniques in Part Two will show you just how to achieve this. For the moment, it is important to see what the tricks are that your mind plays.

All these delusions are created in much the same way. You meet a particular situation, and you smoke. From then on, you have a desire to smoke whenever you are in that situation again. You smoke the cigarette, which satisfies your desire, and you tell yourself a story about how the cigarette helped you with the situation. Tell yourself that story over many years and you have a powerful delusion that you need to smoke in that kind of situation.

Delusions are also held in place because, when you first stop smoking, you experience withdrawal. For example, you will probably lose concentration during withdrawal, so smoking does improve your ability to concentrate in as much as it keeps you from experiencing a withdrawal symptom. It will help you to remember that withdrawal is a temporary phase: when it is over you will be able to think more clearly.

The Miracle Drug

If you study the delusions you can begin to see how ridiculously varied and even contradictory they are. You may tell yourself that smoking wakes you up in the morning and also believe that it helps you get to sleep at night. You simultaneously believe that smoking helps you concentrate and that it distracts you from thinking about something unpleasant. You believe that smoking stops you from feeling hungry and also that it helps you to digest a meal you have just finished. Smoking seems to alleviate both boredom and stress. It's a mask to hide behind when you are unsure of yourself and a social tool to bring people together. It energises and relaxes you.

If you saw a product advertised claiming to do all these things, wouldn't you be just a little bit suspicious? The fact is that you can believe that smoking does almost anything you want it to.

Or, you can honestly admit that all your dependency is an illusion and that the only thing that smoking really achieves is to satisfy your desire to smoke.

This is the truly empowering aspect of stopping smoking. You discover that you really are capable of doing all kinds of things which you previously thought you owed to nicotine.

Magnificent Myths

Here are some of the most common delusions about smoking and some of the facts behind the myths.

□ **Control of powerful emotions**   You might believe that if you stop smoking an uncontrollable rage or desperate sadness will become unleashed. If this seemed to happen in past attempts to stop smoking, it was certainly the result of feeling deprived. In other words, you believed that you couldn't smoke any more, and you got angry and/or sad about that. But if you stay in touch with your choices, the negative emotions disappear, without smoking.

Remember, though, that you made an association with smoking whenever you got upset, angry, frustrated or depressed. So whenever you feel such strong emotions, you will have an intense desire to smoke. When you feel angry, lighting a cigarette satisfies the desire, and you think that it has calmed you down.

In fact, far from calming you down, it excites your nervous system for a few seconds, making your heart race and your head swim. You use the buzz to distract you from whatever it is that is upsetting you, and tell yourself that smoking helped. But distraction isn't particularly helpful. All it does is delay your natural ability to deal with the upsets in your life. You don't need to smoke a cigarette in order to take a few moments to gather your thoughts about the upsetting situation. Assuming that you do not have a sense of deprivation, you will find that you are perfectly capable of dealing with your anger at least as effectively as you normally do, without smoking.

The same applies to depression. If you ever felt depressed

as a smoker, then you know from your own experience that smoking doesn't cure depression. If anything, it makes it worse because you get depressed about your smoking. And the stress smoking puts on your body drains your energy, which further depresses your state of mind.

The solution lies in expecting the inevitable desire to smoke, which, admittedly, will be tough to deal with while you are angry or depressed. It's tough, but it's possible. If you can experience, just once, your anger or depression passing anyway, even without resorting to smoking, then you have begun to overcome your delusion, and accepting the desire will become increasingly easier.

It's important to see that smoking doesn't really help; that you will have the desire, but that *smoking just satisfies the addiction. It doesn't satisfy you.*

You will also feel your desire to smoke, by the way, when you are feeling wonderful. Seeing smoking as a way to celebrate something or increase a sense of happiness is an equally powerful delusion.

□ **Oral gratification**   This phrase is particularly insidious because it sounds like a valid, scientific description of some deep instinctive need. If you take it literally, the term simply means that you stick something in your mouth (oral) and you like it (gratification).

Whatever your addiction, you will always make a positive association with anything that's directly connected with getting your fix. If you were addicted to cocaine, you would become especially fond of sticking things up your nose. And heroin addicts actually get a thrill out of sticking needles in their veins.

However, most people using oral gratification as an excuse are thinking of some far more essential need, apart from and deeper than the addiction or the superficial pleasure.

The theory behind this need for oral gratification, and what appears to give it authority, is the Freudian one that if a baby isn't weaned properly, it will forever after need a substitute. In other words, you can blame your mother for your smoking! But, as many mothers know, two babies can be nurtured in exactly the same way and one of them, as an adult, may end up smoking (or over-eating, drinking, gambling, etc) while the other one doesn't.

A variation on this belief is that sucking on cigarettes compensates for a lack of love or support in your present life. It's so easy to blame your circumstances; *if you resent the circumstances of your life enough, you can justify doing almost anything.*

But if you look around, you will see that there are other people in the same, or worse, situations who don't smoke, and they are coping with the difficulties they face each day. The only difference between you and them is the addiction that you have developed.

Cigarettes aren't your friends. They don't provide you with support; all they support is the addiction.

It may be that you are not happy with things that are happening in your life, and it may be that some of those things are beyond your power to change at present. Your smoking, however, is something that you always have the ability to control completely, no matter what anyone else says or does. In fact, it may be the one thing at this time that you *can* change — and the sense of achievement that you get from stopping smoking could take you on to making changes in other circumstances.

Another belief you may hold is that you need to smoke for the same, unresolved reasons you gave yourself when you first started to smoke, many years ago. And you may think that you need to discover what those reasons are and resolve them before you can successfully stop smoking.

But the important factor is *that* you chose to smoke, not *why*. All that is relevant to you now, in the process of stopping, are the reasons you give yourself now as to why you *continue* to smoke. These reasons may or may not be the same as the ones you gave when you started.

□ **Relaxation and energy**   You get home after a hard day's work and you sit down in your favourite, most comfortable chair with a drink and a cigarette. Smoking has helped you to relax and unwind after the day's hectic pace.

But has it? You have inhaled the lethal gas carbon monoxide in a concentration 600 times the safe level in industry. Along with that you have also inhaled 4,000 chemicals, many of them poisonous, including hydrogen cyanide, carbolic acid and arsenic trioxide.

Nicotine itself is a deadly poison and can be used as an insecticide. If you took the nicotine from one packet of cigarettes and injected it into your blood stream, it would kill you. That's why, with every cigarette you smoke, your heart pounds away about twenty extra beats per minute. Part of the buzz effect that you like so much is your body trying to cope with a poison that is constricting your blood vessels.

Smoking is a cause of stress, not a relief. The delusion that it helps you to relax also comes about through association. Wanting to relax or take a break triggers a desire to smoke. Smoking relieves the desire and gives you the impression that it helped you to relax.

This delusion often gets reinforced during attempts to stop smoking. If you feel deprived when you stop smoking you will fight your desire and you may attempt, or actually manage, to repress it. Either way, you end up more tense than when you were smoking, and of course the problem is alleviated as soon as you light up a cigarette.

The solution is to change the way you are thinking, as part of the process of stopping smoking. Choose to accept your desire to smoke, and go along with it rather than fight it.

The end result, after you have stopped, will be that you feel more relaxed.

You will also, of course, end up with more energy because your body will be healthier, with normal levels of oxygen in your blood. The nicotine buzz makes your heart race and seems to give you energy. But it is not genuine energy, it lasts only seconds and then the effort expended and the chemicals ingested drag your energy level right down.

☐ **It gives me something to do**   Many smokers are concerned about what they will do to occupy themselves when they stop smoking. But this need not be a problem if you are willing to feel and accept the desire to smoke that lies behind it.

When you stop, there will be many gaps during your day where you would have smoked a cigarette. Your concern about these gaps is really your concern about feeling your desire to smoke. Your desire to smoke can be experienced in the form of wanting to pick up a cigarette in your hands and hold it, or wanting to fill an awkward or boring moment.

In fact, there is nothing particularly fascinating about

smoking a cigarette. And your hands don't actually need to be occupied all the time. Just look at all the times during the day when you are not smoking: what do your hands do then?

The Placebo Effect

The truth is that all the help that smoking appears to give you springs almost entirely from the placebo effect. A placebo is something that creates an effect, but the effect doesn't come from the placebo, it is created by your mind — as the following experiment demonstrates.

A group of fifty-six medical students were given either pink or blue pills containing nothing but sugar and told that they had been given either a stimulant or a sedative. Of those who took blue pills, seventy-two per cent decided they must have been given sedatives because they felt drowsy. Pink pills had less of an effect, although thirty-two per cent of those who took them felt less tired, so they concluded that they had taken stimulants. Only *three* students reported that the pills had no effect at all. One third of the students reported side effects which ranged from headaches, dizziness and watery eyes, to abdominal discomfort, tingling extremities and staggering gait. (1)

If these reactions are made spontaneously to a completely inert substance, how much more likely it is that you will attribute extra capabilities to a drug like nicotine, which does have some chemical effect.

An interesting, but probably unanswerable, question is: where does the chemical effect stop and the placebo effect begin?

Certainly smoking immediately produces a faster heart rate, higher blood pressure and more adrenalin. A variety of other effects, ability to concentrate and memorise, for example, have frequently been examined, but so far no clear scientific evidence has appeared to support the belief that nicotine is a genuine aid to human life in any way.

Whatever it is that nicotine really contributes, other than satisfying an addiction to nicotine, is obviously fairly insignificant.

On the other hand, of course, smoking is frequently a

nuisance and can hinder just as often as it seems to help. It takes up time and energy, and is inevitably something that you continually need to think about and cater for. As a smoker, you are obliged to continue smoking at regular intervals in order to keep yourself from going into withdrawal. Far from being a crutch to assist you, it's really more like a ball and chain.

In other words   *IMOGEN*

I had smoked for ten years and given up many times, always returning after a few months when miserable, under stress or in a crisis. I hated and despised myself for smoking and felt my continual return to it meant that I was weak and despicable.

What I liked about Full Stop was that it carefully focused on smoking and the tricks we play with ourselves to stay addicted. Clearly separating out these smoking processes from all the other stress and distress in my life was a revelation and a relief.

Now, when I feel the urge to smoke I don't say 'No, I musn't have a cigarette'. I simply apply the technique. I am now acutely aware that all smoking a cigarette does is satisfy a desire to smoke, it doesn't actually help me feel better or solve a crisis.

The feelings of achievement, control, choice and empowerment are a continual source of pleasure to me. Many people have little sense of their own power, their ability to make choices and to act on them. An awareness of the fact of choosing to smoke or not can begin to release people from their self-imposed prisons and to encourage them to take a more assertive, proactive and positive approach to life.

References

1.   Skrabanek, Petr and McCormick, James: *Follies and Fallacies In Medicine* (1989). Tarragon Press.

8 *THE MOTIVATION TO STOP*

'For thy sake, tobacco, I would do anything
but die.'

Charles Lamb, *A Farewell To Tobacco*

A fundamental goal that all of us, as living things, have
in common is the goal of staying alive and in good
health. Most of the primary functions of our minds and our
bodies are, in fact, orientated towards helping us to survive
and to live full lives.

Like most goals it is not reached in a single bound. An
aeroplane doesn't fly in a straight line. It actually flies in a
series of narrow zig-zags. The plane veers off course, and is
continually being corrected back on course again. Where
the goal of our personal health is concerned, an addiction
interferes with and distorts our natural process of course
correction.

As a smoker, you will have already received lots of signals
indicating that you are off-course: a cough, a sore throat,
loss of energy. These signals call softly at first and, unless
you make the necessary course correction, they eventually
get louder and louder: chronic bronchitis, chest pains, high
blood pressure . . .

The more you ignore the signals, the more off-course you
become. When you wake up with a smoker's hang-over and
'cure' it by lighting a cigarette; when you notice that your
toes are numb from bad circulation and you go on smoking
anyway; when you promise yourself you'll stop smoking
next New Year's Eve, but you don't: all these result in a
stronger and stronger commitment to that altered course.

Let's say that a plane leaves London for New York, and
instead of heading south-west, it flies toward the south. The
longer it takes for the correction to be made, the further
away from its destination it gets. If this plane was a typical

smoker, it would reason that it would be much better to get to Sydney, Australia, before making any changes!

This is what you are doing when you put off stopping smoking. Slowly but surely, you reinforce your addictive behaviour by your procrastination. And the fundamental goal of your own inner health and vitality is bypassed and ignored.

Some Popular Excuses

Usually, smokers rationalise by saying that they are not motivated to stop, or not motivated enough. *But what will it take for you to become motivated to stop?*

Perhaps you are waiting for the addiction to go away, for the day when you wake up and don't feel the desire to smoke any more. But, as explained in Chapter Two, the desire to smoke doesn't go away. In fact, it gets more reinforced the longer you go on smoking. Some smokers find that smoking becomes less and less enjoyable, and even get to the point when they don't *enjoy* it at all, yet this still doesn't cancel out their addictive desire.

Perhaps you are waiting for some event to occur that will provide your motivation. Or until you have sorted the rest of your life out, whatever that may mean to you. But the only time you will be finished with that is when your life is over. Even more dangerous is to wait for your health to deteriorate to the point where you decide that you *have to* stop. As we saw in Chapter Four, this kind of motivation is extremely threatening and because of the additional pressure it actually makes it more difficult for you to stay stopped.

The idea of waiting passively for motivation to stop is a delusion fostered by your addictive thinking.

It is often said that before anyone can successfully stop smoking, they must be completely convinced that they want to stop. That is a myth that keeps people smoking for decades.

What is true is that most smokers deny the real seriousness of their situation, and inevitably approach stopping smoking with a lot of ambivalence. That's where much of the characteristic difficulty about stopping comes from. You are not completely sure that you want to stop, and you are not completely sure that you will be able to stay stopped. These two uncertainties often mix themselves up in your mind. You fear that you will never stay stopped, so you try to accept your life of smoking by telling yourself (and anyone who asks) that you don't really want to stop.

In the early stages, fears about dependency also get in the way of your motivation. If you fear that you will not be able to think clearly without cigarettes, then it will be hard to consider stopping at the risk, say, of losing your job. If you think that stopping smoking will make you put on a lot of weight, continuing to smoke may seem to be the preferable option. If you also feel deprived when you stop, your self-pity will mask any benefits you may gain.

The truth is, you are attempting to do something that is both vitally important to you, and quite challenging, with no way of knowing whether or not you will succeed.

It may be that it is only when you begin to overcome these concerns that you will be able to appreciate that living without smoking is a better way of life for you. But you can only overcome them by stopping smoking and handling the issues in the process.

So, when it comes to stopping smoking, don't make the mistake of waiting until you feel like doing it. You may be waiting for a very long time.

Even if you felt anything like enthusiasm for stopping smoking at first, you will probably not allow yourself to feel it fully: partly because you are not sure how long it will last, and partly because being too enthusiastic might make you feel obliged to stay stopped. At the same time, somewhere deep inside, you may be quietly delighted that you are, at least for now, not smoking.

Or, you may be one of the few smokers who find it almost impossible to feel motivated to stop in any way. Obviously, you need to have *some* interest in stopping smoking, but be reassured — you don't need to feel like a cheer-leader in order to succeed. If you handle the process of stopping correctly, your motivation to stay stopped will develop in time, quite possibly after periods of serious doubt and much debating with yourself.

A Gift to Yourself

If your motivation to stop smoking primarily comes from someone else telling you or asking you to, a consequence tends to be that you hold them responsible for what you are doing. What you are saying, in effect, is: I don't care about my own well-being, but I'll do whatever you want me to do. This inevitably leads to feelings of deprivation sooner or later. You experience stopping as a process of self-sacrifice or martyrdom, with consequent irritability and loss of any effective motivation you might otherwise have had.

It's very likely that you have, in fact, been asked to stop smoking by someone else, but that doesn't mean that this has to be your motivation now. What will work best for you is to put those people who want you to stop aside, in your mind, and focus on the reasons you have to stop that are for you and you *alone*.

This applies whether it's your parents, children, spouse, friend, employer or just society in general who want you to stop.

That is why I advised at the beginning of the book not to tell anyone that you're planning to stop, and to keep it quiet for as long as you can.

I suggest you make stopping smoking a selfish thing that you are doing for your own benefit. By 'selfish', I don't mean that it will take anything away from anyone else. What I mean is that it's something you are doing to please yourself.

This can be difficult, especially for the generation of older women who may have been brought up with the idea that they must always put others first. You might spend all your time looking after others, and think that the one thing in your day that you do for yourself is to smoke. It will be essential for you to see stopping smoking as your own personal choice to gain your own personal benefits, so that you don't end up feeling martyred. Stopping smoking may well be the first 'selfish' thing that you have ever done in your life.

One problem in stopping for others is that your ability to stay stopped becomes dependent on your relationship with those people. Any time they do something that upsets you, your motivation to stay stopped disappears. If you are stopping solely because your employer has made your working environment a no-smoking zone, you will be more likely to smoke when you are not at work, perhaps smoking more in the evenings and at weekends. If you stop smoking so that your children won't be passive smokers, you will be more likely to smoke when they're not around. If you stop smoking at your boyfriend's request, then you will stay stopped up until the time you have an argument with him.

Another problem with stopping for someone else is that, even though they may be people that you love dearly, you can build a resentment towards them because you react emotionally as if they have taken away your cigarettes and forbidden you to smoke.

On the other hand, when you stop primarily because *you* have decided to make this change, you are taking responsibility for yourself, your own health and your own actions. You don't react as if someone has forced you into it. And you don't end up feeling deprived.

It is only if you stop smoking primarily for selfish motives, because it will result in an improved way of life for *you*, that you can get motivated and stay motivated, because staying stopped is now aligned with your own profound inner instincts for survival.

'I Might Get Run Over By a Bus'

Think for a moment about why you are prepared to stop smoking for someone else, but not for yourself. Why is it that they want you to stop, when you apparently don't? How can it be that you are content to go on smoking, but can't bear the thought of your children starting? And how can you possibly wish that someone else that you love would stop, while continuing to smoke yourself?

This is all possible because of an important aspect of the addiction: your well-practised ability to justify your own smoking. All the time that you have been smoking, you have been bombarded by information about the dangers of what you are doing to yourself.

Most smokers defend themselves, both to themselves and to others, by creating a kind of mental buffer. It helps you to live with your addiction in the face of overwhelming evidence that it is one of the most self-destructive things you could be doing. You rationalise, hold beliefs which sound logical, but are, in fact, completely flawed, and you simply deny the more obvious truths.

The rationalisations and denial will be familiar to you and the realities they cover up will be essential for you to face up to as part of the process of stopping. Here are some of the most common. As you read them remember that the key to seeing through any of these lies is to remind yourself that you can always be a smoker, if that is what you *choose* to do with your life.

□ **'The damage is already done.'**   This may well be true in very advanced stages of serious diseases, such as lung cancer or atherosclerosis. But your risk of getting smoking-related diseases like cancer or heart disease declines steadily after you have stopped. And if you already have emphysema, then, when you stop smoking, it won't get any worse and whatever breathing capacity you have, you'll keep.

When people justify their smoking this way, what they may really be saying is that they have given up on themselves. This, of course, is a profound decision. And it is one that you can reverse.

□ **'We're all going to die sooner or later.'**   For smokers, it's sooner. According to a recent study made by the American Cancer Society, 'People who quit smoking before the age of fifty have half the risk of dying during the next fifteen years, compared with continuing smokers.'

If you are fairly young, it's possible that old age doesn't look particularly attractive to you. But as a smoker, you don't eliminate old age, you make it happen sooner. Smoking ages you more than anything else does, both in your external appearance and your internal health.

Yes, you might get run over by a bus tomorrow; nobody knows how long they will live. One thing that you can be completely sure of, though, is that the quality of your health is already impaired, right now, by your smoking. The longer you smoke, the more serious that impairment will become.

□ **'I must have one little vice.'**   Many people are able to stop drinking or can diet successfully, but think of cigarettes as their last straw to clutch on to. But you don't need to have any addictions at all: they serve no real purpose.

The 'last straw' kind of rationalisation often comes from people who are doing a lot for others and spend too little time looking after themselves. If you can see that smoking isn't really a way of looking after yourself, perhaps, after you have stopped, you will want to find other ways of providing real support and rewards for what you do.

□ **'Smoking doesn't affect me, and I would stop immediately if it ever did.'**   Smoking is affecting you now and it's only a matter of time before you will be made aware of it. For some people, the very first symptom that they ever notice is a heart attack. But smoking was affecting them long before that happened.

Another form of denial is pretending that a symptom like shortness of breath is caused by something else, such as asthma or allergies. One way to challenge the pretence is to stop smoking for a while, and see what difference it makes.

As one doctor put it: '. . . addicts are usually unaware of their disturbance of judgement; thus many smokers will allege in all seriousness that their cough is due to damp, draughts, dust, fumes, infection, chill, "catarrh" or gas in the last war. They will take all manner of useless medications while rejecting and even resenting the suggestion that smoking might be responsible.' [1]

According to the US Surgeon General's report of 1990: 'It is safe to say that smoking represents the most extensively documented cause of disease ever investigated in the history of biomedical research.'

□ **'I don't really smoke.'**   This is an excellent example of basic denial. A thirty-a-day smoker, who was terrified of getting cancer, admitted to me that she was able to deny to herself the fact that she smoked. Fortunately, it has now really become true for her. This gives you some idea of the power of the mind to deceive when it comes to justifying addiction.

Many smokers lie to themselves — and others — about how much they smoke and few want to keep track of how many years it has been since they started.

The Experience of Being an Ex-smoker

This list will help you to identify some of the specific ways in which the quality of your life improves after stopping.

Health statistics are a helpful and accurate source of information about the dangers of smoking, but your own experience will be far more relevant to you. It's important to remember what it was like to be a smoker, and exactly what it cost you, in all kinds of ways.

It will be helpful for you to make a detailed list, so that you can refer to it if you forget. Keep it somewhere safe — in this book or in a diary — because you might want to read it through much later on when you could be taking things a bit for granted.

Some frequently reported personal benefits are:

□ More energy
□ Improved sense of taste and smell
□ Improved breathing
□ Improved hearing
□ Improved voice
□ Clearer, less irritated eyes
□ Cleaner, healthier teeth and gums
□ Fresher breath
□ Clearer thinking
□ Feeling more relaxed
□ Less sleep needed
□ Wake up feeling better
□ Improved blood circulation: warmer fingers and toes
□ Improved blood pressure
□ Fewer headaches
□ No sore throat
□ No wheezing or smoker's cough
□ No more pains in chest or legs
□ Better chance of a longer and more active life
□ Much lower risk of emphysema

- ☐ Much lower risk of circulatory problems
- ☐ Diminished risk of many cancers, especially lung, larynx and oral cavity
- ☐ Lower risk of stroke
- ☐ Later onset of osteoporosis (brittling of the bones)
- ☐ Less risk of gastric and duodenal ulcers
- ☐ Less heartburn and acid indigestion
- ☐ Lower risk of pneumonia and bronchitis
- ☐ Reduced risk during a general anaesthetic
- ☐ Lower risk from other drugs and medications, such as contraceptive pills
- ☐ Fewer allergy and sinus problems
- ☐ Fewer and shorter colds
- ☐ Improvement in existing problems such as asthma, diabetes, and emphysema
- ☐ Later onset and fewer problems during the menopause
- ☐ Lower risk of male impotence
- ☐ More satisfying experience of sex
- ☐ Improved sports performance
- ☐ More active and productive
- ☐ More money
- ☐ Better job opportunities
- ☐ Better insurance rates
- ☐ Freedom from restrictions on smoking
- ☐ Cleaner home and car
- ☐ No burnt clothes or furniture
- ☐ No more smelly ashtrays
- ☐ Less risk of starting a fire
- ☐ Safer driving
- ☐ Great sense of accomplishment
- ☐ No more fears about the consequences of smoking
- ☐ No more guilt about smoking
- ☐ No longer obsessed with the need to stop smoking

☐ Freedom from dependency
☐ Increased self-confidence and self-respect
☐ No longer smelling like a smoker
☐ No nicotine stains on fingers
☐ Looking younger
☐ Improved complexion
☐ Fewer wrinkles
☐ Improved scar healing
☐ Feeling in control
☐ Desire and confidence to make other positive changes
☐ More positive view of life

This is *not* a complete list! There is, for instance, a large number of serious physical conditions that smoking either creates or makes worse. There is no part of your body that smoking does not affect because it keeps high levels of poisonous chemicals in your blood stream, and blood supplies every cell in your body. This happens with every cigarette you smoke, from the first cigarette you smoked. It's just a matter of time before the symptoms get dramatic, but smoking affects you long before that.

The difference in the healing of scars is interesting because it is so easily measured. A study was made of a group of women undergoing the same minor routine operation. The group of 120 included sixty-nine smokers. After healing, the smokers' scars were almost three times as wide as that of the non-smokers. (2)

Can You Expect Immediate Results?

There is, of course, no way to guarantee that you will get *all* the benefits that you hope for straight away. Sometimes, for example, people anticipate having more energy when they stop, and are disappointed to find that doesn't seem to increase much at all. This actually depends on your level of fitness. Smokers who engage in sport or regular exercise almost always find that their endurance improves after they stop smoking. They can easily measure it in terms of laps swum or squash games played and won. Often, those people who say that they don't feel any fitter are not at all fit to begin with. Stopping doesn't make you fit; although it does improve your ability to increase your level of fitness.

The speed of improvements in health will also depend on how much you've smoked, and for how long. The more damage done, the longer it will take for your body to recover. Different bodies react in different ways: some people feel very much better from the day they stop and others take a very long time, perhaps six months, before they can notice any improvement in their health.

But of all the benefits of stopping, the most commonly felt that my clients tell me about is derived from feeling free from dependency, and this happens almost at once. They experience an enormous thrill from being in control of their addiction for the first time in years.

Many people also gain benefits from stopping that they are surprised by. When I stopped smoking, I was very surprised by how much more alive I felt in the mornings. One recent client was surprised that her chronic lower back pain disappeared within a week of stopping. Another, after thirty-five years of smoking, was surprised by the smell of a pencil.

It is important, however, especially in the first few weeks of stopping, to look honestly at the difference not smoking is making to you and to remember honestly what smoking was like. In particular, don't underestimate the peace of mind that you will have when you are free from the habitual fear and guilt you have lived with as a smoker.

Finally, if you really don't see any improvement in your life at all, remember that you can always go back to being a smoker. I have almost always found that whenever anyone truthfully considers the options open to them, they soon get in touch with their real motivation to stay stopped. You might decide that you really do want to be a smoker — just remember the rest of the package that goes with this deal. It's up to you!

In Part Two, we will describe in detail how to work with the benefits that apply personally to you, to support you to stop, and stay stopped for good.

In other words　　　　　　　　　　　　　　　　　JANE

I remember my first cigarette well. I was fifteen, on holiday in Scotland and lit up a St Moritz menthol complete with gold band to impress Stuart from Glasgow — a glamorous creature of eighteen or so. Stuart was unmoved, but I had taken my first step towards a sixty-a-day romance with smoking which was to last for twenty years.

In all that time I never even tried to give up smoking. I loved it. It gave me 'confidence'. It was 'sophisticated'. Bedridden with bronchitis I still managed thirty a day and it was an unusual Saturday night that did not involve a 4am trek to some distant all-night store to replenish supplies.

I went to Full Stop as a journalist, just as an observer with no intention of giving up and a sceptical view of the claims made for the course. One week later I was an ex-smoker, still a doubtful one, but I had passed my first twenty-four hours in a decade without a cigarette. And as one smoke-free day led to another I had to concede that perhaps I really had stopped.

Three years later I still haven't smoked and, though I still experience the occasional desire to do so, I am astonished by the relative painlessness of the process. That Full Stop truly works is borne out for me by the fact that I had not passionately wanted to stop — and had never for one moment thought that I could anyway. Full Stop is a remarkable technique that took me by surprise.

References

1. Johnston, L., Tobacco Smoking and Nicotine. *The Lancet* (1942) p.742.
2. Siana, J. E., Rex, S. and Gottrup, F. The effect of cigarette smoking on wound healing. *Scand. J. Plas. Reconstr. Surgery* (1990). 23:207–209.

PART TWO
A SKILL YOU CAN LEARN

9 CHANGING YOUR MIND

> 'Reason does not work automatically; thinking
> is not a mechanical process . . . The function
> of your stomach, lungs or heart is automatic;
> the function of your mind is not. In any hour
> and issue of your life, you are free to think or
> to evade that effort.'
>
> Ayn Rand, *Atlas Shrugged*

Now that you understand the nature of your addiction and just how powerful it is, Part Two will focus on the practical aspects of how to train your mind to accept and deal with your experience of wanting to smoke. These techniques are aids to changing your thinking. They won't do the work for you: they are tools for you to use.

It's helpful to understand how the techniques work while you are still smoking, so it's a good idea to read through these chapters before you stop. But you can only learn to use it after you have stopped because it's impossible to deal with your desire to smoke effectively while you are still satisfying it with cigarettes.

As with any other skill, like swimming for example, a certain amount can be explained first, and then there comes a point when you can learn no more until you face your fears and get into the water.

The first step is to recognise that even after you stop smoking, you will still need to handle your desire to smoke. These are your only options: you either go on smoking, or you learn how to deal with the desire.

The desire will fade in time, becoming less and less frequent, and much less intense. But it's not the infrequency of your desire to smoke that will help you to stay stopped. What makes the difference in the long term is how you deal with it when it's there. *The process of stopping smoking is the process of learning how to deal with your desire to smoke.* Your mind needs to be *consciously* retrained by you.

Outlined here is everything that you need to know in order to handle your desire for a cigarette whenever it occurs. While you are smoking, your desire has been connected, thousands of times over, with smoking a cigarette. Now, a new connection is being established: your desire to smoke becomes your cue to think.

The Outline

Step One: 'I have a desire to smoke.'
As soon as you are aware of a desire to smoke, begin by saying these words to yourself. It does not mean that you want to go back to being a smoker. It simply enables you to identify what is happening in your mind, and by noticing it, gain some time for yourself to choose what to do next.

Step Two: 'I am free to smoke!'
This reminds you that you really have a free choice. If you don't actually remind yourself of this, the addicted part of your mind will assume that you can't go back to smoking and will immediately start to create symptoms of deprivation.

Step Three: 'One puff, and I'll be smoking.'
Word, by word, you spell out the simple truth: you are always just a puff away from connecting with the full force of your addiction again, as we saw in Chapter Six.

Step Four: *Either* 'I choose to return to smoking,' *Or* 'For now I choose to accept this desire rather than smoke.'
Now, there's a choice for you to make. Try saying to yourself 'I choose to return to smoking', and see if it's what you really want to do. Alternatively choose to accept the desire.

Choosing for now is a reminder that you are making a choice that will not last for ever. You accept the desire just as it is right now, even if it feels very uncomfortable. The more times you can experience the desire to smoke and choose to accept it, instead of reacting by smoking, the easier it will become to do this.

If you want to, you can use the word 'welcome' instead of 'accept'. 'Welcoming' the desire to smoke means that you accept it completely and unconditionally. Chapter Eleven explains why this is the best approach to take.

Step Five: 'I'm choosing this in order to gain these benefits . . .'
Finally, complete the process by reminding yourself of the benefits to you in stopping smoking. Which is the most significant to you might change from day to day. Chapter Eight will help you to get further with this part of the technique.

Here is the whole process outlined in one sequence:

The Outline
(How To Make A Choice)

Step One:	'I have a desire to smoke'
Step Two:	'I am free to smoke!'
Step Three:	'One puff, and I'll be smoking'
Step Four:	

Either:	**Or:**
'I choose to return to smoking'	'For now, I choose to accept this desire, rather than smoke'

Step Five:	'I'm choosing this in order to gain the benefits of . . .'

Making It Real for Yourself

It's important that you really consider each of the statments in the Outline. It's common to have doubts about them at first, because you are still in the process of changing the way you think. Spend time thinking about them. Just saying the words parrot-fashion, without any conviction at all, won't help you in the longer term.

In order to help you make the Outline authentic, I suggest, as I suggest to all my clients, that you *carry your cigarettes with you at all times* during the first couple of weeks after you stop smoking. Don't hide away from the reality of your desire. Instead, have packets of your favourite brand around you as much as possible, with matches, lighters and ashtrays, just as they usually are; at work, at home and when you are socialising. Have an open pack of your cigarettes right in front of you, whenever you feel the desire to smoke, and if possible hold it in your hands.

Some people like to talk to the packet, holding a dialogue with their addiction. It's as if the addiction is talking to you, and in order to stay stopped you need to learn how to talk back to it.

The more uncomfortable you feel about carrying cigarettes, the more resistant you probably are to making the necessary changes in your thinking. When you have real cigarettes in front of you, you will face real, intense desires to smoke, and then you will be able to reinforce the choice and the freedom to smoke in a real and lasting way.

Carrying cigarettes is the part of the technique that some clients object to most strongly when they first hear about it, but later say it is the part they appreciate the most. It makes an enormous difference, because it quickly breaks down the panic, anxiety and misery of thinking you are being deprived. It's the best and fastest way to become genuinely confident that you can be in control of your addiction, and stay in control.

The main objection to carrying cigarettes, of course, is that in a weak moment you might smoke one without thinking. But if you stop smoking with cigarettes at hand, you can overcome your fear that your desire to smoke will overpower you. Understand that it's not your desire to smoke that makes you smoke. It's the inevitable consequence of your *unwillingness to accept the desire.*

Finally, if your ability to stay stopped depends on not having any cigarettes within reach, then you aren't going to stay stopped for long. You are living in a world full of cigarettes, people are going to be smoking them, even offering them to you, and there is no doubt that you will have some desire to smoke them.

This is from a study of relapsed smokers: 'Other smokers serve not only as cues for smoking but as sources of cigarettes. In half of all relapsed episodes, another smoker provides the cigarettes that are smoked . . . in most cases the ex-smoker specifically asks for a cigarette.' [1]

Unconscious Smoking

Using the Outline will help you deal with your desire to smoke in a way that gives you conscious control over your smoking, without any side effects, and without the danger of starting again unintentionally.

As a smoker you may smoke in an unconscious way quite often, completely unaware that you have lit a cigarette, while you had your mind on something else. It's common and entirely understandable to expect that this might happen after you have stopped.

If you were to try and stop by repressing the desire, it would be easy to find suddenly you have lit a cigarette, and you may even have done that in the past. This is because you never trained your mind to acknowledge and accept your desire. The repressed desire lived on in your subconscious, and drove you to smoke, automatically. There was no possible way for you to be in control of what you were doing.

You will find that it's virtually impossible to smoke unconsciously if you have stopped smoking using this technique. It would only be possible in a case where someone is still heavily repressing everything, despite the method. Chapter Eleven explains how to induce the desire, which will be an essential technique if you have a tendency to repress.

When you stop smoking by acknowledging and accepting your desire to smoke, your conscious mind soon gets accustomed to noticing and dealing with it.

At first, however, you may find yourself reaching for a cigarette completely forgetting, for the moment, that you have stopped. But you will find it's impossible to get one in your mouth and light it without realising. When you are a smoker, smoking another cigarette in an endless line of thousands is a relatively insignificant thing for you to be doing. After you have stopped smoking with this technique, however, lighting a cigarette becomes very significant.

An entirely different kind of unconscious smoking is the smoking that you may be doing in your dreams. It's quite common, after you have stopped, to dream that you are smoking and wake up unsure whether it really did happen. This can be upsetting at first, but a great relief when you realise that it was only a dream.

Dreaming about smoking doesn't mean that you are not handling things effectively in your conscious, waking life, and it certainly doesn't indicate that you are going to relapse. All it means is that smoking is very much on your mind.

The Line of Most Resistance

When it comes to stopping smoking, you can expect resistance all the way: it's part of the process. Before you stop, you might try to think of every excuse under the sun to go on smoking just a little bit longer. When you do stop, and you begin to work on staying stopped, there are a few more tricks your addicted mind can come up with to resist making any real changes.

□ **Forgetting the Outline**   It's quite possible that you will completely forget a line or two of the Outline. The addicted part of your mind resists acknowledging the truth by simply blanking it out. This is one reason why it's important to say the Outline over and over again, not just to understand the theory behind it.

You might want to write the Outline down and keep it with you at all times during the first few days of not smoking. You could keep it with your cigarettes. Then, if you have forgotten what to say to yourself, you can always read it.

Eventually you will want to memorise it so that you can think it through at any time. Your desire to smoke will come and go, and you will always know how to cope with it when it's there.

☐ **Changing the Outline** A more subtle piece of resistance is to change the wording of the Outline by saying: 'I choose not to smoke'. When you make choices 'not to smoke', you do not define what it is that you *are* doing. You could, for example, manage to not smoke for a while by resenting or even repressing the desire to smoke. It is important to remind yourself that the way you stay stopped is to make choices 'to accept the desire'.

☐ **Believing you are too busy** Resistance also comes in the form of deciding that you are 'too busy' to think about your desire to smoke. If you are a busy person, it will be important to make stopping smoking a priority for the first few weeks.

This means deliberately taking the time to deal with your desire to smoke. It takes less than thirty seconds to go through the whole Outline, very carefully. You will find that it is actually easier to keep taking the time to deal with your desire, than to push it aside. You will be and feel much more in control if you make a clear choice to accept it each time.

If you keep using the technique, it will work: if you don't use it, you can find yourself in difficulty.

If you find that you are feeling your desire to smoke during a conversation with somebody, on the phone for example, then first of all finish the conversation. Then, at the earliest opportunity, think through the Outline to yourself before you start anything else.

It's a mistake to tell other people what you are thinking and feeling when you have a desire to smoke: make it your own decision to accept your desire. It can be helpful to say the Outline out loud if you are alone, but my advice is to deal with your desire privately, especially at first while you are integrating the technique into your everyday life.

How to Recognise the Desire

The desire to smoke is first of all a thought, which then becomes a physical sensation. You might find this hard to believe at first because the desire is so persistent and because there are other sensations during withdrawal (created both in your mind and in your body) which get confused with the desire. But even after a couple of days, it should become obvious to you that the desire is triggered in your mind by events and circumstances, and not by a physical need.

Even though it is created in your mind, the desire is experienced as a physical sensation that leaves you feeling quite uncomfortable. You may well notice the physical sensation before the thought, but a thought always precedes it. When you first stop smoking, it feels like a wave of discomfort all over your body. Later on, after you have stopped for a while, it can be similar to that sinking feeling you get when you realise, for instance, you've locked your keys in the car.

Different people feel their desire to smoke in different ways, in different parts of their bodies. You might feel it in your chest area or throat, remembering the feeling of the smoke going into your lungs. You might feel the desire in your stomach and confuse it with hunger, or it may be more like wanting to put something into your mouth. Some people salivate more than usual when they want to smoke.

The form of your desire can change from day to day. In general, as times goes on, it will become less of a physically uncomfortable feeling and more like a thought. If you let yourself have these uncomfortable feelings and thoughts, then you will be able to stop smoking and stay stopped for good. If you don't, you won't: it's as simple as that.

It will be very much easier for you to accept when you remember that you are *choosing* to feel it, because, as far as you are concerned, it is better than the alternative of a life of smoking. This is just as important to remember months after you have stopped as it is when you are in withdrawal.

In other words   *IRENE*

I had previously tried to stop smoking by cutting down gradually over a period of time. I realise now that I was trying to get rid of the desire — and why I was so unsuccessful! I thought at first that these techniques would also help me get rid of the desire and that because I was still having these feelings I couldn't be using the Outline properly. I'm one of those people whose pain threshold is very low and I'll do anything to avoid it and protest loudly if I can't. Among other things, what the Outline requires is that you accept the pain! This idea had never occurred to me before. For me, it made all the difference when I acknowledged the desire instead of being frightened that I would immediately have a cigarette. In other words, I had a choice.

What helped the most was when I treated the desire — the voice nagging at me to have a cigarette — like a little child who needs attention. All the child needed was not to be ignored but to be given sympathy, love and attention.

References

1.   The Health Consequences of Smoking: Nicotine Addiction. (1988) US Department of Health and Human Services.

10 STARTING STOPPING

'Think of me as one, even when four months
had passed, still agitated, writhing, throbbing,
palpitating, shattered; and much, perhaps, in the
situation of him who has been racked . . .'

Thomas de Quincey, *Confessions of an English
Opium Eater*

WITHDRAWAL is your transition from being a smoker to
being an ex-smoker. It is usually the most difficult
part of stopping smoking, and the first question you
probably have is: when will it end? You may have heard
various estimates — from two days to four weeks — and
there is no one answer that applies to everybody.

First of all, it depends on how much you have smoked,
and for how long. In general, if you have only smoked for
five years you will experience less withdrawal than if you
have smoked for fifty. There are, however, always indi-
vidual variations.

How long withdrawal lasts also depends on how you are
dealing mentally with the process of stopping. Symptoms
that are the result of physical changes become magnified
and prolonged by your mind, so that what would have been
a temporary problem becomes a persistent threat to your
ability to stay stopped.

The most convincing proof of this comes from studies of
smokers who experience the symptoms of withdrawal even
though they have nicotine in their systems because they are
using nicotine gum. (1)

The duration, intensity and variety of symptoms are
essentially a reflection of how resistant you are to changing
your thinking in the process of stopping. So how long
withdrawal lasts is very much up to you.

Let's take a closer look at the symptoms that are the result
of physical changes, not influenced by your state of mind.

The Physical Withdrawal

□ **Feeling light-headed, dizzy and disorientated** This is mostly due to the presence of a great deal more oxygen in your blood than you are used to, and it's actually a sign that your circulation is improving. The carbon monoxide in cigarette smoke inhibits your blood's ability to carry oxygen and the resulting increase in blood oxygen levels after you stop smoking is most noticeable in your brain. Occasionally this may affect your ability to think and concentrate clearly. This effect is variable from person to person, but for most people it starts to improve after the first day or two. By then your brain has readjusted to the new levels of oxygen, resulting in significantly *increased* mental alertness.

□ **Tingling sensation** If your circulation has been badly affected by your smoking, you may feel tingling sensations, especially down your arms and legs, for a day or two after stopping smoking. As nicotine constricts your blood vessels, your blood flows more freely when you stop smoking, and this change sometimes feels strange at first.

□ **Constipation** This can be a serious and persistent problem for some ex-smokers. Nicotine artificially stimulates the action of the bowels, as many smokers know, and some people have come to rely on smoking as the way to 'get them moving'. Over a long period of time, the bowels depend more and more on nicotine, so the ex-smoker becomes constipated.

□ **Tension and difficulty getting to sleep** Another physical side effect of getting nicotine out of your system comes from the fact that caffeine has a stronger effect on you and stays in your body longer. If you feel tense after you stop smoking, try cutting down on your caffeine intake, and see if that makes a difference. If you have difficulty getting to sleep, try decaffeinated drinks in the late afternoon and evening. Note that coffee, tea and many soft cola drinks all contain caffeine, and they are all available in decaffeinated forms. Many pain-killers and pre-menstrual medications also contain high levels of caffeine.

□ **Increased sensitivity to alcohol** Alcohol can also have a stronger effect on you, so that you get tipsy faster on less.

Some clients of mine report this effect to begin with, and a few tell me that it seems to be a permanent change.

□ **Excess catarrh** Your nose can run because your sinuses are draining properly for the first time since you started smoking. Also, you can cough up nasty stuff from your lungs. Unpleasant as it seems, these are both signs of your improving health.

□ **Bad taste** Some people experience a nasty taste in their mouth when they first stop smoking. This same taste was there when you smoked: when you stop smoking, your taste buds come back to life and so you become aware of it.

□ **Sore throat** Your throat may feel sore when you first stop. Smoking makes your throat sore, but as it also numbs your whole sinus area, you only begin to feel it after you have stopped.

If these kinds of symptoms are very persistent, they may be more significant and you should consult your doctor.

The Mental Withdrawal

The fundamental and potentially most problematic symptoms of withdrawal come from the ways in which you react mentally to your unsatisfied desire to smoke.

When you first stop smoking, assuming that you are not avoiding or repressing, you can expect your desire to smoke to be fairly constant for about two days. For some people it's continuous and for others it comes and goes in waves. The second day is often more intense than the first.

During this time, you may also be quite disorientated, so you end up feeling rather peculiar, to say the least. After these two days (variable from person to person) you will see the desire begin to diminish.

The people I have worked with who just experience their desire, and nothing else, are willing to accept it as a temporary phase and don't see it as a problem. It doesn't have to feel like hell.

Problems arise if, when they feel the desire for a smoke, people tell themselves they have been *deprived* of the chance to satisfy it.

If you feel any of the following *symptoms of deprivation*

after you stop smoking, then you have not yet changed the way you are thinking:

□ **Desire to smoke doesn't diminish** Your desire becomes exaggerated because the one thing that you think you 'can't' have is the one thing that you want the most. Even a week after stopping you still feel strong desires for hours on end, and are pining and full of self-pity about having stopped.

□ **Anger and resentment** You feel frustrated and martyred, get angry and blame the whole world for having to suffer this torture.

□ **Depression** You can get depressed (which is really a form of repressed anger) because you react as if something that brought joy into your life has been taken from you for ever. Many common withdrawal symptoms are nothing but symptoms of depression: loss of energy, apathy, early morning waking and inability to concentrate and make decisions.

□ **Anxiety** You feel like a caged wild animal: you become restless and anxious. In extreme cases of deprivation, anxiety can reach a state of panic and symptoms of panic attacks are possible: palpitations, difficulty in breathing, dizziness, hot and cold flushes, sweating and trembling.

□ **Tension** You resent feeling the desire for a cigarette because you believe that you have no choice about it so you fight and resist it, which creates tension: aches in neck, shoulders, and stomach, and symptoms such as nausea and difficulty relaxing and, therefore, sleeping.

□ **Stress and Hunger** Yet another product of deprivation during withdrawal is repression. The desire doesn't simply disappear. It is an energy that is being 'bottled up', and it will eventually emerge in some other form: nervous energy, psychosomatic symptoms of stress (whatever is your Achilles' heel), and, most frequently, ravenous hunger.

Getting Free, Staying Free

Freedom is a basic requirement of all people. It is more important to you than almost anything else, certainly more important than stopping smoking. If, after you have stopped, you don't feel *genuinely free* to smoke, then you will feel deprived until you get free.

It's essential to discover what it is that leads you to conclude that you *can't* smoke. Some of the beliefs which give rise to feelings of deprivation are covered in Chapter Four, and you might identify with one or more of these. Or, you may have your own, unique circumstance which leaves you feeling convinced that you don't have a real choice about this. If it is particularly difficult for you to overcome this issue, here is an exercise you can use to identify the thinking that supports your false belief:

Step One   Take a piece of paper and if you are still smoking, write down: 'I have to stop smoking because . . .' and complete the sentence with as many different endings as you can think of. For example: '. . . if I don't, I'll die.' Or: '. . . otherwise I will hate myself.'

If you have stopped smoking, and are feeling deprived, write down: 'I can't go back to smoking because . . .' and finish that sentence in as many different ways as you can. For example: '. . . if I do, I will have failed.' Or: '. . . if I do I'm afraid I'll never stop again.'

Leave one line blank in between each sentence. Be creative and find as many endings as possible, even those that seem outrageous or absurd.

Step Two   This is the crucial step, because it liberates you from your false belief. Go over your sentences, examine every line, and remind yourself that *you are still free to smoke anyway.* The reasons you have listed are the consequences that you get, or might get, from choosing the option of smoking; they do not mean that the option of smoking does not still exist. Write this in on the lines you have left blank.

For example: 'If I don't stop, smoking might kill me, but I still could go on smoking.' Or: 'If I go back to smoking, I will have failed in my attempt to stop, but I'm still free to do that.'

The very act of writing it down will be highly effective in reinforcing this new thinking.

Smoking is not an advisable choice, it's a disastrous option for you to take and quite possibly one that you desperately hope you don't take. But that never means it's not an option that is always available to you.

Focus on choosing *only for the present time*. Consider that most of the resistance to getting in touch with your freedom to smoke is your fear that if you really *can* smoke, then you will! (Go back to Chapter Five if you want clarification on the value of making choices *only* in the present time.) This is especially helpful during the withdrawal phase. The more you make choices only for now, the less deprived you will feel, because then you are keeping your options wide open.

The simple key is to remember that you are totally free to smoke, and *you don't have to do it to prove it*.

You Only Withdraw Once

Withdrawal is an essential first step to stopping smoking. For most smokers it is quite a challenge and it's helpful to have realistic expectations about it. If you think that it will be, or that it should be, effortless and easy, then you may very well be in for a surprise. But if you prepare yourself for a challenge, and if you are prepared to deal with all the deceptions that your addicted mind will produce, then you will emerge from the withdrawal phase successfully, and find staying stopped easier and easier to do.

Be encouraged by the fact that, if it is dealt with correctly, withdrawal is a temporary, one-off event. As soon as the changes have been made, both physically and mentally, they are over and done with and you will never need to go through anything like that again.

In other words   **BRIAN**

I remember my first cigarette. I was in the woods of the local golf course with three or four other fifteen-year-olds. The first drag made me feel sick and giddy. But, like an idiot, I stuck with it and pretty soon I was indeed stuck with it — a twenty-five-a-day habit that would, over the following twenty-three years, cost me thousands of pounds, make me smell revolting, and give me a wheeze that sounded like the mass pipes of the Royal Navy.

I'd tried giving up just once, on National No-Smoking Day. By eleven o'clock I was a wreck. By ten past I was smoking. So I trotted out the usual smokers' excuses: it's the pressure of my work . . . I don't really smoke that many . . . it's just something to do with my hands . . . I couldn't have a drink or a meal without a cigarette.

At first I was wary of the Full Stop programme. I figured that it was just a mind game, a trick. But reluctantly I started to focus on the choice that comes with every cigarette, eliminating the automatic flipping open of my pack of Rothmans. Did I really want to go on smoking? Wouldn't I prefer to give up coughing and wheezing? I started to deal with my habit one moment at a time. Logic entered into a subject that had always been dealt with on an emotive basis. I started to feel in control. The first few weeks were tough, but recognising that feeling uncomfortable was a critical and positive part of the quitting process made all the difference.

Now, some three and a half years later, the choice of whether to smoke or not arises far less frequently, and has become much easier to deal with. I don't feel smug — just pleased. I'm in control of my life and I'm not smoking — not at the moment.

References

1. 'Of particular interest was the continuance, apparently unabated, of increased hunger for at least four weeks . . .'
    West, R., Hajek, P., Belcher, M: Time course of cigarette withdrawal symptoms during four weeks of treatment with nicotine chewing gum. *Addictive Behaviors* (1987) 12:199–203.
    'Withdrawal symptoms were less reliably alleviated [by nicotine gum]. These included depression, anxiety/tension, difficulty concentrating, restlessness and the urge to smoke.'
    Nicotine Addiction: The Health Consequences of Smoking US Department of Health and Human Services. Report of the Surgeon General (1988). p.208.
    'Five symptoms — dizziness, alertness, frustration, feeling miserable, and disorientation — were not affected by nicotine relative to placebo.'
    Pomerleau, O.F. and Pomerleau, C.S. *Nicotine Replacement: A Critical Evaluation.* (1988) Alan R. Liss, NY. p.116.

11 *TAKING CONTROL*

As a smoker wanting to stop smoking, you are in a state of conflict. On one hand, you have an addictive desire to smoke. On the other, you want to stop feeding it. Stopping smoking and staying stopped depend on resolving this conflict correctly.

As soon as withdrawal begins, your conflict may be deep and last for several hours. You may question yourself over and over again, asking yourself if you really *do* want to stop smoking, and whether this really is the right time to do it. You may spend hours trying to figure out a good excuse to justify smoking for just a little bit longer, or just one more . . .

Don't be surprised by this: it's all part of the process. The way through this conflict is to experience it and then resolve it, and not avoid it in any way.

The basic question to ask yourself is: *Am I willing to accept my desire to smoke in order to stop smoking and stay stopped?*

Out of Sight, But Not Out of Mind

Some people avoid resolving this conflict by repressing their desire and quite often feel confident that they have conquered their addiction. One of the more unhelpful things about repression is that, at the time you use it, it appears to be effective, and is therefore rarely perceived as being a problem.

If you have ever stopped and gone back to smoking, the act of picking up a cigarette and lighting it was preceded by a desire to smoke, even though you may have only been dimly aware of that desire at the time.

James, who attended a recent course of mine, gives us a dramatic example. He told me that at his last attempt, three years ago, he decided to stop smoking at the same time that he was going to redecorate his house. In other words, his strategy was to *avoid* as much of the difficulty of stopping smoking as he could by keeping busy painting and hanging paper.

He threw his cigarettes away and got rid of anything that might remind him of the smoker he used to be. The plan appeared to work and he managed to completely repress his desire to smoke. He stayed stopped for a month, with smoking totally forgotten, until something happened that took him by surprise.

He told me that he was at the station where he commuted to work each day and went to the kiosk where he always used to buy his cigarettes. He asked for chewing gum, but the man behind the counter, recognising him, handed him his usual packet of cigarettes.

James took them, paid for them, opened the packet, took out a cigarette, lit it and was half way through smoking it before he realised what he was doing. He was simply not aware of the desire to smoke that was guiding his actions. When he realised that he was smoking he felt devastated, but the damage was already done: he had gone back to smoking again, and was soon smoking his usual number of cigarettes.

When you stop smoking by repressing your desire to smoke, you have no way of controlling your automatic reaction once the desire finds a way to break through.

If James had spent that whole month consciously dealing with his desire to smoke, then, when he was given cigarettes by mistake at the station, he would have noticed there was a desire to smoke, and used the Outline to deal with it.

Learn to Induce the Desire

If, like James, you have stopped smoking in the past by

repressing your desire, then you may well continue to do so automatically whenever you make an attempt to stop.

The best way to check yourself is by deliberately inducing your desire to smoke, so that you can retrain yourself to deal with it and consciously accept it. This might look as though you are making things more difficult for yourself, but in fact you are simply facing up to the difficulty that already exists.

Inducing a desire to smoke is a conscious mental exercise. It means deliberately interrupting your thoughts about the other things in your life, and, with your cigarette packet in front of you, focusing on the feelings inside you of wanting to smoke.

There is a reason that the desire is being repressed in the first place: you are resentful and afraid of it. When you deliberately induce it, you break down your resentment and fear, and turn the desire into something you have power over.

If you find inducing the desire difficult you will need to be creative. Watching other smokers light cigarettes can be helpful. Smelling your cigarettes in the packet or, if you used to make your own, rolling one up should produce the desire to smoke. For some people, imagining that they are smoking is the best way to feel their desire to smoke. If you are really stuck in repression, buying a new pack of your favourite brand and taking the cellophane off may do the trick.

Sometimes people flirt with smoking, testing their limits to the point of putting a cigarette in their mouth and lighting a match. Obviously, this is a dangerous game to play, and, by the way, a game that indicates that you feel forbidden to smoke. It's not necessary to go this far: just looking at cigarettes in the pack should be enough for you to get in touch with your choice and desire to smoke them.

What you are doing is making a connection with the memory of your addiction: the memory stored in your mind, which thinks that smoking would be wonderful. Adverse thoughts will also be part of that memory, but don't use them to 'cancel out' your desire because you need to work on accepting the desire, not denying it.

Some people will repress their desire to smoke from the

moment they stop smoking. In that case, you will need to pause frequently, perhaps three or four times during each hour, and induce a desire you can really feel. It may take a while to work, but eventually you will feel a strong desire: an uncomfortable sensation that you know would be relieved by smoking.

For other people, repression only becomes a problem a few days or weeks after stopping. What happens is that the desire is so intense at first that it is impossible to repress it, but as it fades in strength, it becomes increasingly possible to ignore it altogether.

After a few weeks of not smoking, you will need to induce your desire to smoke only a couple of times in a day, but it's just as important to do so because it's only while you stay in touch with your desire to smoke that you can stay in control of it.

Take familiar smoking situations, such as the end of a meal, as opportunities to induce your desire. Instead of jumping up from the table to get on with the washing up, sit there for a while, as you would have done, and let yourself feel your desire to smoke.

Later on, your desire to smoke may only last a few seconds, but making a deliberate effort to acknowledge it by inducing will make the difference between success and failure in the long term.

If you lead a very busy life, inducing your desire will be especially important. Busy people can stop smoking for days or weeks, barely aware of their desire to smoke in the background of their busy minds. But just because you don't take the time to deal with it properly, the desire doesn't vanish, it keeps coming, like a nagging child demanding attention. Or, the desire can suddenly and unexpectedly explode, perhaps at a time of crisis, and because your conscious mind hasn't practised dealing with it, you can suddenly find yourself on the verge of smoking.

If you stop to induce a desire — and this only takes a few moments — you give your desire the attention it requires. As a result it becomes easy to live with and, most important of all, you are in control of it.

The Benefits of Inducing

It's difficult to describe how effective this is. At first glance, the idea of inducing desires to smoke can seem perverse and masochistic: why tease yourself with temptation if what you really want to do is to never smoke again?

The reason is your memory. Just because the desire, and perhaps the cigarettes, are out of sight, they cannot be truly out of mind, because of your memory. By inducing, you learn to accept that part of your memory — the desire to smoke — whenever it becomes activated. If you use this technique, you will see for yourself how well it works.

When you first stop, you can expect to feel your desire to smoke at least as often as normal, in situations where you would have smoked. If you are in a situation where you never smoked — in a cinema for example — then don't try to induce. But make sure that you feel and deal with your desire as soon as you leave that situation, if that's the time you would have smoked.

To begin with, the more you feel your desire to smoke, the better. Inducing the desire to smoke is a very effective and powerful technique, and any time you use it — whether you think that you are repressing or not — you will not be going wrong.

I have seen, through working with hundreds of smokers over many years, that those who use the technique of inducing their desire have an extremely high chance of success in the long term.

As time goes on, you will need to induce the desire less often but if you keep inducing it from time to time, your chances of staying stopped are excellent.

Why Welcome a Desire to Smoke?

Welcoming the desire to smoke is entirely the opposite of resisting it. When you welcome it you embrace and entertain it, becoming totally hospitable to this sensation of discomfort. *You make it your friend instead of your enemy.*

Each desire will inevitably pass in time: you don't get

permanently stuck in a state of desiring to smoke. But the crucial move is to accept it while it's there. There are a number of reasons for this, and it's important to understand them in order to be able to welcome something that is genuinely uncomfortable.

Your natural reaction will be to resist feeling uncomfortable: this is human nature. If you are too hot, you open a window. If there's a stone in your shoe, you take it out. Always, you are attempting to maintain a state of comfort. This is basically an appropriate self-correcting mechanism that helps you maintain a state of well-being, in as much as you can.

With an addiction, however, this natural instinct for seeking comfort gets in the way. This is because, when it comes to breaking free from an addiction, the feeling of discomfort is something that you need to experience above all else.

Feeling the discomfort is part of your healing process, your recovery from addiction. Anything you do to get rid of it is equivalent to the act of smoking again. Therefore, you need to deliberately intervene, to over-ride your natural instincts, and remind yourself that, in this instance, discomfort is good for you, because while you are feeling it, you are not smoking. As a direct result of feeling the discomfort of your desire, the quality of your life will be improved. It may even, quite literally, save your life.

Your mind won't welcome discomfort automatically. You need to consciously retrain your thinking to see the value in it.

Remember that when you welcome the desire to smoke:

□ You are saying, in no uncertain terms, that you'd much rather feel this discomfort than go back to being a smoker.

□ You overcome your fear of it. When you welcome the desire nothing will make you smoke. This way you can quickly become confident, in all kinds of situations and even under extreme stress.

□ You can look at it objectively and see through the delusion that smoking 'helps you to cope'. This is because you learn to see it as nothing more than just another desire to smoke. Smoking simply satisfies it — nothing else.

□ It releases any tension (physical aches and nervous energy) you might otherwise build up in your fight against feeling uncomfortable. It's like walking into a gale, and then changing direction so that the wind is behind you. When you welcome the discomfort, you are going along in the same direction.

When I say 'welcome' I don't mean to imply that you should enjoy it. Occasionally, some people do tell me that they enjoy feeling their desire to smoke, but most people don't. It is genuinely uncomfortable; welcoming it means that you view it as something of value. *Welcoming it means unconditional acceptance, and it gives you absolute control.*

You can see the discomfort as a payment, or a trade-off. By being willing to feel this temporarily uncomfortable sensation, you receive the benefits of not smoking. As a direct result of feeling the desire, you have more energy, greater self-respect, you feel cleaner and younger, you save lots of money and no longer live with the fear and guilt that smoking inevitably creates.

I have worked with a few people who refuse to take this step. They stop smoking, but then they maintain that either way they go, they lose. Either they return to smoking, which they don't want to do. Or, from time to time, they feel their uncomfortable desire to smoke, which they don't want to do either. They hang on for a while, continuing to resent and resist their desire, even though it diminishes to a few moments of discomfort each day. Before long they return to smoking, with another failure behind them and even more resistance built into their minds.

The difference between success and failure in stopping smoking is not physical. It all comes down to your willingness to accept feeling temporarily uncomfortable in order to gain the benefits of not smoking.

Your Freedom to Choose

If you do choose to smoke, of course, you return to smoking, satisfying your addictive desire with one cigarette after another. You reinforce your addiction, and run the risk of never stopping smoking again. If you remind yourself of your options in this way, by going through the Outline with every desire to smoke, the alternative of accepting a few minutes of discomfort will soon seem more attractive, and will continue to be the alternative you are most likely to choose.

It will help you to put the discomfort into the correct perspective. It is not torture. It is not a fate worse than death. It is just a temporary discomfort. It's intense at first, but it does diminish. At first you may only just be able to accept the uncomfortable desire, but as it diminishes after the first couple of days, you can work towards welcoming it positively so that you fully resolve any conflict and resistance you may have towards it.

When you can be sure that you would rather feel your desire to smoke than live your life as a smoker, you have every chance of long-term success.

I have found that welcoming the desire is usually the very last thing that people really understand about this technique, and some people never do! Those who do welcome it are the most successful in the long-term, because of the simple fact that the desire to smoke never does completely go away.

In other words   BARBARA

I started smoking at the age of sixteen, although it wasn't until I was about nineteen that I became a heavy smoker, roughly twenty a day. Over the course of twenty years I smoked sometimes thirty cigarettes a day, and am ashamed to say, continued puffing through both of my pregnancies. I tried to stop smoking, or cut down as much as I could, but to no avail.

To be quite honest, I never dreamed that I would be able to stop, but four years have passed now, and I feel so much better. My skin doesn't have that sort of yellowy look!

The most helpful thing that I learned from Full Stop was the technique of holding the cigarette packet during those first few days of giving up. I can remember ironing with one hand, while the other clutched the cherished cigarette packet. Even now I use the techniques in my mind to overcome the feeling of wanting to smoke.

The best thing about not smoking is feeling better, no more tenseness around the neck and shoulders, and not feeling reliant on something that is not natural. Also, the theatre and cinema outings are more enjoyable now. As a smoker I would be looking anxiously at my watch, waiting for the interval to arrive. The feeling of freedom from all of that is like a weight lifted from my shoulders.

The most difficult time I have experienced since stopping was when my father was critically ill, in intensive care. However, he fully recovered I'm glad to say, and by using the Full Stop method I managed to get through it as well!

This is the only positive way to stop smoking. You can do it, with determination and the knowledge of these techniques.

12 *MOMENTS OF TRUTH*

'It is in this whole process of meeting and
solving problems that life has its
meaning. Problems are the cutting edge
that distinguishes between success and
failure. Problems call forth our courage
and our wisdom; indeed, they create our
courage and our wisdom.'

M. Scott Peck, *The Road Less Travelled*

Because most people don't want to feel their desire to smoke after they have stopped, they often try to avoid any circumstance that has a strong association with smoking. They reorganise their lives as much as they can, so that they will be faced with temptation as little as possible.

If someone goes to a particular pub regularly, then they avoid the pub when they stop smoking, staying home in the evenings instead. If they used to smoke at work, they might decide to stop smoking while they are away on holiday, to avoid facing their working day without a cigarette.

Parties, friends who smoke, coffee breaks, demanding work, restaurant dinners and long journeys are all typical situations that ex-smokers fear and often go to great lengths to avoid during the first weeks, and even months, of not smoking. And you may find that you consider this path to some extent.

The most obvious problem with this kind of strategy is that it is totally impractical to try to avoid all the situations that may trigger a strong desire to smoke. You cannot avoid everything that might be stressful, upsetting, enjoyable, demanding or boring, to name just a few examples, unless you just stop living.

But, even if you do manage to eliminate most of these situations from your life, what is it that you are really avoiding? It's not the situation. You have coped with those countless times and have no special fear of them. What you are trying to avoid, of course, is the desire to smoke you know you will face.

While following this strategy of avoidance might appear to help you with stopping smoking initially, it certainly won't help you to stay stopped. It's actually one of the biggest factors that explains why people don't stay stopped.

When you deliberately avoid the potentially more difficult situations, what are you really doing is accepting your desire to smoke only *conditionally*. You establish, in your mind, that you will accept your desire to smoke, and thereby stay stopped, *provided* you are not with any smokers. Or, *provided* you're sober. You'll do it, *provided* you're not upset. Or *provided* you're not bored, tired or under any stress. And, above all, *provided* your desire to smoke is not too intense, or persistent.

Unfortunately, your addiction doesn't strike bargains. And if you ever try to make a compromise with it, you end up the loser.

The desire to smoke will continue to reappear from time to time in all kinds of circumstances, long after you have stopped smoking. This is inevitable. The only strategy that is going to keep you from smoking, in the long-term, is for you to be willing to accept feeling it sometimes, no matter where you are and no matter what is going on.

The way to stop smoking and stay stopped for good is to come to an unconditional acceptance of your addictive desire to smoke, and to do it as soon as possible after you have stopped smoking.

In certain circumstances your desire to smoke will be more intense and persistent. These are the circumstances where you have developed a stronger dependency on smoking. It's understandable that you will be concerned about whether you will get through them without smoking. What will make all the difference is how you cope with this fear, right from the beginning.

Remember from Chapter Five that you can stop worrying about an approaching situation by staying in the present. You can only accept your desire to smoke at the time you are actually feeling it, so don't even try to predict what you will do. If you avoid the situation, however, you reinforce your fear by giving it more credibility.

If you avoid a difficult or tempting situation, you cannot possibly break from your dependency. You can only do this by going into each situation, learning how to handle it without smoking, and dealing with your desire to smoke at the time.

Does this sound like needless torture? It's not. What would really be needless torture would be living in fear of being overwhelmed one day by an intense desire to smoke. Needless torture would be trying to make changes in yourself and your life in the hope that you will eliminate your inevitable desire.

Needless torture is stopping smoking, but not doing anything to break your psychological dependency, and so going back to smoking over and over again.

Keep to Your Routines

First of all, you need to know whether or not you are about to avoid anything when you stop smoking. In order to do this, just ask yourself: *'Would I be doing this if I hadn't stopped smoking?'* For the first couple of weeks, as much as possible, stay with what you would have done as a smoker (except smoking!).

□ **Social situations**   Go to the pub or to parties, just as often as you always have done. Be there as you usually would, with a drink in your hand and everyone smoking around you. Think through the Outline to yourself and make private choices to accept your desire because, as far as you're concerned, at least for now, you prefer to be someone who doesn't smoke.

□ **Daily routines**   Follow all your normal routines as a smoker, exactly as you used to do. Notice any changes you might be thinking of making, however innocent or well-intentioned they appear to be.

Let's say that you feel like taking your dog for a walk one evening, a day or two after you've stopped smoking. Ask yourself what you would be doing if you hadn't stopped smoking? If you *normally* walk your dog each evening, then go ahead and do it.

If, however, you don't, then it's likely that you are in fact wanting to avoid something: perhaps a half-hour of sitting around with not much to do before dinner? You would have been smoking, and your sudden interest in your dog's exercise is really nothing more than your avoidance of your desire to smoke.

□ **Places you smoked** Don't avoid the places where you used to smoke — your favourite chair, desk, kitchen table. If your house is a no-smoking zone, you may have stepped out to the porch or garden whenever you wanted to smoke. To begin with, take your usual trips to the garden, with your cigarettes, and make your choices to accept your desire to smoke there.

□ **At work** If you used to smoke at work, your first working day after you have stopped smoking can be quite a challenge, because you may well have the kind of job where demands are constantly being made on your attention.

It's realistic to assume that you won't be working at your best for the first few days, because of the constant distraction of wanting to smoke. But the more you take time to deal with your desire to smoke, the sooner things will get better.

By far the most effective approach is to pause, mentally, at least a couple of times during an hour, and focus directly on your desire and deal with it by thinking through the Outline.

This doesn't make the desire go away: it's not supposed to. But when you remind yourself of your choices and make a clear choice to accept or welcome the desire, then you will find that you can return your attention to your work and continue for a bit longer.

If your work is very hectic, you may need to plan special strategies so that you can take this personal time with your own mind. You could pretend that you are reading something for a few moments, or, as a last resort, take yourself off to the toilet.

You probably have special routines at work when you would go to a particular place to light up a cigarette. It might be someone else's office, a coffee room, the toilets or outside the back door. For at least the first week, *make sure you don't avoid any of these. Take as many breaks as you normally would, go to those same places, take your cigarettes with you, and deal with your desire to smoke!*

Some people say that they are just too busy to do this, or that their work is too important and too demanding to spend so much time thinking about smoking. It's a matter of choosing to make stopping smoking a number one priority for a while, and in the long run your work will benefit.

An addicted smoker is a less efficient worker; buying and smoking cigarettes takes up time, you can get distracted during meetings where you are not allowed to smoke, you get more tired and stressed because of your smoking, and need more time off work due to smoking-related illness. (1)

If you decide that you are too busy to spend any time dealing with your desire to smoke, it might be more honest for you to admit that it's really because you just don't want to bother.

Many people make the fundamental mistake of thinking that if they hang on long enough without smoking, things will improve by themselves. I wish it were true, and I should think that a great many relapsed smokers do, too. What happens if you keep pushing your desire to smoke to one side is that you can end up feeling tense, frustrated and disorientated. Also, you might be able to avoid feeling your desire all day at work, but get hit with it on your way home. Or, you might be able to ignore it for a week or two, but then return to smoking at the very first crisis that comes along.

☐ **Concentrating**   A common result of not dealing with the desire is that you become unable to concentrate properly on anything at all, and the longer you avoid dealing with this, the longer your lack of concentration will go on, continuing for weeks and even months. Your work may require you to concentrate on writing, for example, and if you simply avoid doing the work, putting it off until you feel more like tackling it, you will end up reinforcing the delusion that you actually can't work without smoking! Which is the perfect 'rational' excuse to resume doing it . . .

The way to break this delusion is to sit down to write as

usual, and *expect to feel* your desire to smoke. The association between writing and smoking has been made, so the desire will be there as an automatic, 'knee-jerk' reflex. Focus your attention on the desire and deal with it, deliberately and carefully, by going through the Outline, making a clear choice to acknowledge it, and accept it. Then, without fighting the desire, bring your attention back to what you are doing.

This will slow you down a bit at first, but even if you write just a little without smoking to begin with, you are proving to yourself, gradually, that your beliefs about your dependency are completely fictitious. It's only when you've discovered that you really *can* write without smoking that you will be likely to stay stopped, and you can *only* do that by going ahead and writing, even though it may look impossible at first. You are re-educating yourself, and at first it might even seem like you are learning to write all over again.

I have worked with a number of professional writers who, through exactly the same process, have learned to continue to write and have also successfully stayed stopped. One novelist client told me that his main problem was more with his fear that he wouldn't be able to write without smoking. As soon as he had written the first piece that looked OK, he felt much more confident, and he has never looked back. Now he is busy with a new novel, and he finds he still occasionally gets the desire to smoke, particularly when he is looking for inspiration. The key for him is in *knowing* that the inspiration will come anyway, without the cigarettes.

□ **If you take other drugs** One of the situations most frequently avoided when people stop smoking is that of drinking alcohol. Your fear (as if I needed to tell you) is that you will not be able to be in control of yourself if you are intoxicated.

As someone who smoked while drinking you will undoubtedly experience a strong desire to smoke whenever you drink, especially at first. But this is nothing more than the same desire which has been triggered into your mind by the conditioned association you created over the years. And you are just as capable of thinking through the Outline and making a choice to accept it as you are when you are sober.

If you usually drink alcohol, *don't avoid it at all when you stop smoking.* Drink as you normally would; drink the same amounts in the same situations, and deal with the desire to smoke as it comes along, in the normal way.

Even if you have had a few drinks, you are still capable of making a choice to accept your desire to smoke. Even when you are quite intoxicated, you still set your own limits to your behaviour. If you know you can draw the line when you want to about other things when you are drunk, like jumping into bed with anyone you fancy, or driving your car, then you can also choose to be in control of whether or not you smoke a cigarette, if you want to.

It's probably not a good idea to get extremely drunk for the first day or two after you have stopped smoking. In fact, if you do, it's more likely to be a problem of substitution (see Chapter Thirteen). But, as with other avoidances, it's going to be much better for you to overcome your fears as soon as possible and face that intense desire to smoke the first time you sit down with a glass of beer or a bottle of wine.

This also applies to taking 'recreational' drugs, such as marijuana or cocaine. Again, the association with smoking cigarettes is strong, but the same process applies: don't avoid it, for the same reasons, and expect and accept your desire to smoke cigarettes, which will be intense at first.

Please understand that I'm not encouraging or advocating the use of any drugs: the two just mentioned are illegal, and, to varying degrees, addictive and dangerous as well. What I am saying is that if you usually take these drugs, don't *stop* taking them *at the same time* as you stop smoking cigarettes. This adds up to an avoidance of the desire to smoke cigarettes, as far as dealing with your addiction to nicotine is concerned.

You may or may not be addicted to other drugs and you may or may not want to stop taking them later on, but this is another matter. When you stop smoking, it's important to deal with that one drug: nicotine. Then, whatever other drugs you may be taking, you will find you are able to stay off nicotine, because you have dealt with it as a separate issue.

When it comes to marijuana, it's easy to get confused, for two reasons. One is that it is usually smoked like a cigarette. But this doesn't mean that it *is* a cigarette, as long as it doesn't have any tobacco (nicotine) with it. You can inhale its smoke into your lungs and still not be smoking tobacco.

The other complication is that marijuana is often mixed and smoked together with tobacco. It's important to be very clear about this. If you make a choice to smoke tobacco together with marijuana, then you are back to your old nicotine addiction again, and you will inevitably return to smoking cigarettes. Tobacco is by far the more addictive drug of the two, and smoking even a puff or two of a joint containing tobacco will sooner or later take you back to smoking cigarettes on a regular basis.

At the same time, *it's essential that you do not substitute any other drugs for cigarettes* in the process of stopping smoking. (See Chapter Thirteen.)

There are many people who use drugs of all kinds, and have every intention of continuing to use them. But it's completely unnecessary to be stuck with smoking tobacco as well.

If this applies to you, understand that you can stop smoking tobacco and stay in control of your addiction to nicotine, if you use this technique with honesty and care. And you can use what you have learned to help deal with other addictions, if you want to, later on.

Continue to Deal with the Desire

As your first week of not smoking goes on, you will start to feel your desire to smoke less often. As it diminishes, it will be important to keep dealing with it as much as possible. Even many weeks after stopping smoking, when you may only feel your desire a couple of times a day, accepting and dealing with the desire will make the crucial difference as to whether you stay stopped or not.

By advising you not to avoid anything, I do not mean that you should never make any more changes in your routines. After the first two weeks, go ahead and make any changes you want. But during that time, if something unexpected comes up and you find yourself doing something you wouldn't normally do, ask yourself: 'Would I have done this if I hadn't stopped smoking?' If the answer is 'No!' then you will know that you are trying to avoid feeling the desire to smoke.

It Gets Easier

Although it can certainly seem more difficult at first, facing all these situations from the very beginning, instead of avoiding them, actually makes things much easier for you in the long run.

The most challenging times can be the most ordinary: sitting at your kitchen table, talking on the phone, driving your car. When you have faced these things *once* without smoking, then, the next time you are in that situation, it will be much easier for you to deal with. And the reason it is easier is because you have created a new memory: a memory of being in that situation without smoking, perhaps for the first time in years. You did it, you survived, and you didn't smoke. And it will be even easier the next time, because the desire will be that bit less intense and that bit less persistent, and because smoking will seem that bit less necessary.

Each time you face the situation, and the resulting desire to smoke, you reaffirm to yourself that you would rather accept feeling the desire than return to smoking. *The more often you do this when you first stop smoking, the greater your chances of success in the long term and the sooner you will break free from your dependency.*

Many people tell me that the circumstances that they were most concerned about usually turned out to be much easier than they had feared. It's actually the surprises that are hardest to handle, precisely because they cannot be anticipated.

Suddenly, without any warning, you walk into an argument, or there's an accident and, inevitably, there's also an intense desire to smoke. There is no way you can avoid these things happening in your life but, if you have been practising dealing with your desire to smoke anyway, you will see your desire to smoke at times of upset as nothing more than just another desire to smoke for you to make a choice about.

Temptations exist, and you will be faced with one, sooner or later. While you are trying to avoid the inevitable desire to smoke, you are not coming to an acceptance of it. You cannot do both, and unless you overcome your fear of your desire to smoke, and learn to accept and deal with it, no matter what situation you are in, you are very likely to return to smoking eventually.

Before attending a Full Stop course almost a year ago, a client named Marianne used to stop smoking regularly, at least twice a year, while staying at a health farm.

She told me that at these times she was very eager to stop smoking and that stopping seemed effortless. Each time she stopped she fully intended to stay stopped, and was genuinely puzzled by her repeated relapses back into smoking either on her return home, or very soon after.

What Marianne needed to learn was that, although she was highly motivated to stop smoking, without training her mind to deal with her desire to smoke (repressed during her health farm visits), she had no way to turn her motivation into real success.

When she learned this technique, she started to face and take control of her addiction in her normal routines, and at the time of writing has stayed stopped over ten months, which is very much longer than she ever did before.

In other words   *TIM*

In truth I no longer believed that I could stop, even if I had really wanted to. So most of the time I did not let myself admit that I wanted to, which made it easier to live with myself.

But there were times when, above all, the fear of the consequences would get to me and I would try almost anything to stop myself wanting a cigarette. Because I associated smoking with all the unhealthy things in my life, I would turn instead to all the things that I associated with health and fitness. So I would go for long, invigorating walks, or take up swimming regularly; I would cycle to work and make plans to join a gym and get myself super fit. I would cut down on alcohol, give up drinking coffee, which I've always accompanied with at least one cigarette, and drink mineral water instead. All together I devised a punitively puritanical regime.

Such resolutions were inevitably ill-fated. Around every corner lurked the demon I was running away from. I would say to myself: 'Let me be fit and healthy, but let me first have a cigarette!'

And then the truth dawned — or rather it was pointed out to me. That there was no necessary connection between all these things. That stopping smoking was simply about stopping smoking: it was not about taking up anything else. All I needed to do was acknowledge that I wanted to smoke, that I was quite free to do so, and at the same time I didn't have to just at the moment. What I had seen as an over-powering menace which had left me feeling defeated and very feeble, was reduced at a stroke to simple, manageable proportions.

References

1. '. . . over fifty million working days were lost each year due to smoking-related illness and the likely cost in terms of lost production was estimated to be between £2,200 million and £3,200 million.' HoC Hansard Col.349W 11/3/91.

13 *YOU DON'T HAVE TO GAIN WEIGHT*

'The objects of desire are like salt water,
The more we enjoy them the more our craving
will increase.'

Tibetan Buddhist saying

THERE have been numerous studies made over the years
to assess the problem of weight gain after stopping
smoking. Recently, the US Centers for Disease Control
published the results of their research into this problem,
conducted over thirteen years of about 2,000 people. It has
been the most comprehensive study of its kind, and the
findings were that, on average, men who stopped smoking
gained 2.8kg (about 5lbs) and women 3.8kg (about 7lbs).
More frightening is that one in ten men and one in eight
women gained 13kg (28.7lbs), or more.

Your metabolic rate does tend to slow down a bit when you
stop smoking, and this can account for a small amount of
weight gain. But by far the greatest culprit with gaining
weight lies in the substitution of food and drink for cigarettes.

Controlling substitution may be complicated by the fact
that you sometimes eat and drink in an addictive way. For
many smokers, the process of stopping smoking is also
about controlling this addictive behaviour as well.

Most people indulge in some addictive eating — which I
define as anything you eat, whether healthy food or not,
over and above what you need to stay alive and healthy.
When you stop smoking, don't even try to eliminate all the
addictive eating that you may do: just make sure that your
addictive eating doesn't increase, as a substitution for
smoking. You will be able to do that if you become aware
of what is really going on.

When you smoke, you satisfy your desire to smoke with
cigarettes. When you substitute, you satisfy your desire to
smoke with food and drink.

The extra calories you consume add up to extra pounds, but substitution isn't just a problem with weight. Substituting anything for a cigarette, whether it contains calories or not, has a damaging effect on your original smoking addiction because every time you satisfy any addictive desire, you strengthen it. When you substitute you are smoking food: *you are making choices equivalent to smoking because you are feeding the desire to smoke.*

This can happen in two ways:

□ You react to the desire to smoke by eating or drinking more. Soon, your desire to smoke can become repressed, covered up by a desire to eat, which you feed.

□ You repress your desire to smoke spontaneously, and experience it in a disguised form: an addictive desire to eat. You don't 'feel like' smoking a cigarette, you 'feel like' you want to eat or drink something. So you feed and reinforce that desire.

Either way, you end up with a persistent addictive appetite that you have developed as a result of stopping smoking.

Of course, the most obvious problem with feeding an increased appetite is one of weight gain, but the really insidious result of substitution is that, while you are substituting, you are not coming to an unconditional acceptance of your desire to smoke. Instead, you are reinforcing it and you may also be repressing it. As a result, quite apart from the problem of the extra pounds gained, a return to smoking is much more likely.

If you are repressing most of your desire it can seem to you that you are accepting it. But you are only accepting what you are aware of, which is merely the tip of the iceberg: most of it has been repressed by the extra eating you are doing. You experience a brief, very acceptable desire to smoke, but also an addictive hunger, which you are satisfying.

As you may know from past experience, the desire to smoke isn't completely satisfied by anything other than a cigarette, so when you substitute, you are feeding an insatiable appetite. The action of feeding the addictive desire keeps the addiction alive. As your addictive appetite gets larger, so do you. Finally, you go back to smoking because you don't know any other way to stop yourself from eating so much.

How to Break the Cycle

This depressing cycle from smoking to over-eating and back to smoking again is an all-too-familiar one. For many smokers, staying stopped for good will only be realistic when a way can be found to control substitution of food for cigarettes. The answer lies, once again, in your acceptance of the desire to smoke.

First of all, it's going to be essential for you to take notice of potential substitutions.

This may seem obvious, but it is one of the most common problems. Eating is a fairly ordinary activity and it's very, very easy to gradually increase amounts without realising it. This is especially likely if you are not a weight-watching, calorie-counting eater in the first place. After you stop smoking, you may need to become much more aware of your decisions to eat, and not just go ahead and eat automatically every time you feel like it.

Remember that you may not feel your desire to smoke; you just fancy something to eat, so you need to find out first of all if what you are about to eat is really a substitute or not.

There is one very effective way to tell if you are substituting, and that is to ask yourself this one question before you eat or drink anything: *would I be doing this if I hadn't stopped smoking?*

If it's something that you usually eat at this time, then go ahead and eat it. If it isn't, then realise that you have a disguised desire to smoke. If you identify it as that, it will be much easier for you to make a choice to accept it rather than feed it.

Now see if you can get in touch with the real desire to smoke that is behind your desire to eat. Take out a pack of cigarettes, and whether you feel it as a desire to smoke, or whether it just stays as a desire to eat, go through the Outline and make a choice to either accept your addictive desire, or to return to smoking.

If you are not sure whether or not you would have eaten

a particular thing at a particular time as a smoker, play it safe, and treat it as a substitution.

It's crucial to see that your desire to substitute is your desire to smoke in disguise, and to deal with it as that. If you don't, substitutions just look reasonable, innocent and even helpful, because they seem to keep you from smoking.

People often think substitution is manic binging. It can be, but it is far more frequently subtle and sporadic. It may be a few biscuits here, and a bar of chocolate there, and an extra helping of casserole at dinner . . . and two stone later you are seriously considering returning to smoking.

When you first stop smoking, expect to have more of an appetite, especially wanting to go on eating at the end of a meal. Expect to want more meals, more snacks and larger amounts.

What will make all the difference is whether you feed this extra desire to eat or whether you decide to accept it. When you feed it, you reinforce it. You satisfy it for the present time, but it comes back again later and rapidly becomes a persistent addictive appetite.

Excuses, Myths and Questions

□ **At least I'm not smoking.** This is a great way to rationalise substitution; eating a few odds and ends here and there instead of smoking yourself to death rationally seems the far lesser of two evils.

But substitution is a short-term 'solution' that creates long-term difficulties. And one of those long-term difficulties is a return to smoking, either because of never-ending, uncontrollable weight gain, or because the repressed desire to smoke suddenly erupts and no amount of substitution gets it repressed again.

□ **I know I'm not substituting, because my clothes still fit me.** It depends a great deal on your size and style of clothes, but it is possible to put on more than a stone before you notice it. Unfortunately, many people only get serious about dealing with their substitution problem after they have got upset about their weight gain.

This makes the whole problem more drawn out, and if you do take this path, expect to feel a stronger and more frequent desire to smoke whenever you do stop substituting, since when you cut back on your eating it will no longer stay repressed.

□ **I'll take the weight off later.** In case you don't know, it's actually a lot easier not to put the weight on in the first place. Maintaining weight is tough enough: losing it is a very slow business.

For example, let's say that you maintain your present weight by eating 1,500 calories a day. Then you stop smoking and substitute, eating 1,750 calories a day for two weeks. You gain half a stone, so you decide to stop substituting and cut back to the 1,500 calories you were eating before you stopped smoking. But that's the amount of calories that maintains your weight, so you don't lose the extra pounds you put on while you were substituting until you cut back a whole lot further.

Also, while you are substituting, the question still remains as to whether you can control the amount you eat without smoking. When you begin the process of stopping smoking by taking control of your desire to smoke, and not substituting at all, you establish for yourself that you can be in control of both eating and smoking at the same time. Sooner or later, you will be faced with that issue anyway, assuming you don't want to become obese. It's much easier to tackle this from the beginning because then you learn to accept the addictive desires, instead of reinforcing them.

□ **My metabolism has changed since I stopped smoking.** Your base metabolic rate is whatever energy it takes for you to simply stay alive: it's the rate at which your body burns up energy. Your heart needs to beat faster when you smoke, so when you stop smoking it slows down, and your metabolism slows down too. The real question is by how much, and how much weight gain will that produce?

Results of various studies on this matter differ widely: some research says that metabolism doesn't change at all, some says that smokers' metabolism is faster only during exercise, but not while resting. The general consensus seems to be that the drop in metabolic rate is about five per cent. [1]

What this means is that if you eat 2,000 calories a day, the drop in your metabolism when you stop smoking will be equivalent to eating an extra 100 calories a day. Or, to put it another way, if you eat 100 calories less than you eat as a smoker, you won't put on any weight at all.

If you don't make this adjustment, your changed metabolic rate might result in a couple of pounds extra weight after a month of not smoking, assuming that you don't increase your level of activity. This, of course, will vary from person to person. So it's safe to say that metabolism plays a very small part in weight gain from stopping smoking.

Some people think that their metabolism slows down dramatically when they stop smoking because they become very constipated. But this isn't caused by changes in your metabolism, which is simply to do with the rate at which your body burns calories.

□ **Nicotine suppresses hunger.** It has been shown that nicotine gum doesn't alleviate hunger at all during withdrawal from smoking. (2) The reason is that most people experience two entirely different kinds of hunger: a natural and appropriate need for nourishment that everybody has and an additional addictive appetite that can be developed to a greater or lesser extent. It can be virtually impossible to tell them apart, especially for someone who over-eats a lot. When you stop smoking, the extra hunger you may feel is not natural, but purely addictive hunger.

Natural hunger *alone* is very easy and even pleasant to live with for reasonable periods of time. It comes and goes regardless of whether you smoke or not.

When someone claims that nicotine suppresses their hunger, all that is happening is that they are satisfying their *addictive* hunger with a nicotine buzz.

□ **I smoke to control my addictive eating.** As a smoker, whenever you felt addictive hunger or just fancied something to eat, you probably either ate something or smoked a cigarette. You fed your addictive desire to eat with something. You got into the habit of smoking instead of eating and then, when you stopped smoking, you switched to eating instead of smoking. The desire to smoke and the desire to eat easily become entwined and interchangeable.

You may see yourself more as an over-eater who smokes, rather than a smoker who attempts to stop smoking by over-eating. The question is whether you really want or need to continue to control your eating in this way.

One thing that you can be sure of is that you can never properly deal with your addiction to food while you are still smoking. You create and maintain a powerful addiction to nicotine *and* you never learn how to really control your addictive desire for food. After many years of smoking, when both addictions are well established, smoking becomes a less and less effective way to control addictive eating: hence overweight smokers.

If you have a serious over-eating problem, stopping smoking will also be a process of learning how to take control of your eating addiction. You may never have done that before without smoking, but it's possible.

Simply apply the same technique of choosing to expect and accept your addictive desire, paying particular attention to staying in touch with your choices. The overwhelming compulsion to eat — that feeling of being driven — always stems from a state of deprivation, so don't forget that you *can* eat as much as you want! You have the choice to over-eat all your life. There are consequences if you do that, but no rules and restrictions, and especially no restriction on your own responsibility for your own actions. Also, identify the delusions you hold about how your addictive eating cheers you up, helps you cope, stay awake, etc.

□ **I have a healthy appetite when I stop smoking.** This illusion can be enhanced by improved vitality and sense of taste and smell after you stop smoking. But just because you have got lots of energy and food tastes better, that doesn't mean that you *need* to eat larger amounts!

You do not have a 'healthy appetite': you have an addictive appetite. There is actually no valid need to consume more food just because you have stopped smoking. If anything, you need less food, because smoking depletes vitamins.

In a very few cases smokers under-eat, and as a result are underweight. In this case, a genuinely healthy appetite will normally be restored after stopping smoking, but it's still wise to be very careful about substitution in the form of addictive eating.

□ **Whenever I eat it seems that I satisfy my desire to smoke. Am I substituting?** When you first stop smoking, your desire to smoke will be very persistent, so it's entirely possible that you will feel as if you are satisfying it any time you eat or drink anything at all.

This is why it's so important to identify substitutions with the question: *'Would I be doing this if I hadn't stopped smoking?'* Don't ask yourself if you are hungry, because you may have a false hunger that is really a desire to smoke, or you may have a real hunger because it's lunch time. Don't ask yourself if you really want to eat or if you really want to smoke, because you may want either or both at the same time.

□ **Is it OK to substitute chewing gum or water?**   Substitution is not just a potential weight problem: it's the choice to feed the desire to smoke, instead of accepting it.

It's also a mistake to think that you can substitute selectively. If you begin to substitute, even a cup of tea or a piece of fruit, you establish substitution as an alternative that you are going to take. Then, you will have an increased addictive desire to eat which you will want to satisfy with whatever food is available at the time, whether you happen to be at a salad bar or in a bakery. This is especially true if you have addictive eating patterns anyway.

□ **For years I have been substituting mints for cigarettes during the day because I'm not allowed to smoke at work. Should I cut these out when I stop smoking?**   No. You can get totally confused trying to figure out whether or not things are substitutions for smoking that you have already established. Just focus on the possible danger of increasing the amount of substitution in the process of *stopping* smoking. If you usually eat popcorn at the cinema, for example, go ahead and do that, even if you only started to do that when the cinema became a no-smoking zone.

□ **Will it help to substitute nicotine gum?**   I use the term substitution to mean something that you do or consume instead of nicotine. In that sense, nicotine gum is not really a substitution: it is simply another way of taking the same drug.

A number of studies have shown that nicotine gum is hardly effective at all when used alone, and has only produced modest success in the long-term when used together with regular group meetings. Of those who do chew the gum and stop smoking entirely, some become addicted to the gum, but the vast majority return to smoking within a year. (3)

Although chewing nicotine gum is certainly less dangerous than smoking, nicotine in any form is a risk factor, especially to the heart, circulation and stomach. Also, nicotine gum frequently produces side effects, including indigestion, nausea, vomiting and hiccups.

Furthermore, nicotine gum does very little, if anything, to break your addiction to nicotine, because while you are chewing it, you are still keeping your addiction to nicotine alive.

If you already use nicotine gum, either exclusively or together with smoking, then use the Outline to deal with your desire for nicotine, in whatever form you take it.

□ **I can't smoke, and now I can't eat either**   Deprivation is the underlying cause of substitution. If you believe that you can't smoke, you are more likely to want to eat to compensate and to reward yourself for the self-sacrifice you believe you are making. If you also believe that you can't substitute either, you will feel very sorry for yourself until you decide to start rebelling, by eating and/or smoking.

The helpful thing to remember about substitution is that you are not cutting out food and drink that you enjoy when you stop smoking: you are simply making sure that you don't *increase* your eating and drinking, so that you can identify, deal with, and continue to accept your desire to smoke. And, you don't *have to* do any of this at all.

You don't need to watch out for substitutions for the rest of your life. Weight gain is, of course, always a possibility, even for smokers, but it's when you first stop smoking and the addictive desire is at its strongest that it's most likely to be replaced with substitutions.

This is the real value of welcoming, not only because you really do take and stay in control of your smoking, but also because, if you unconditionally accept your addictive desire to smoke, you won't need to cover it up with any other compulsive behaviour.

If you follow this technique, your weight gain when you stop smoking, if any, will be slight.

In other words   *CATHY*

My weight is now around nine and a half stone and I have not put on any weight since giving up smoking. I do remember wanting to eat more in the early days, and using the question: 'Would I be eating this if I was still smoking?' I believe that without that I would have eaten a lot more. One day in particular I felt haunted by a bar of chocolate I had in the fridge and I used the Outline a lot that day. I remember that it was tough, but I stayed with it and conquered it. Looking back on it now, I can see that day was a major turning point for me. I did have more desires to smoke after that but I knew it was up to me, it was my choice. I love knowing that, and until now, more than three years later, I haven't smoked. Full Stop is one of the best things I have ever done for myself.

References

1. Nicotine Addiction: The Health Consequences of Smoking (1988) US Department of Health and Human Services.

2. See Reference 1, Chapter Ten.

3. 'One of the more reliable findings about nicotine gum has been that it is only marginally efficacious, if at all, when prescribed in the absence of a context for behavior change.'
    Pomerleau, O.F., Pomerleau, C.S. *Nicotine Replacement: A Critical Evaluation.* (1988) Alan R. Liss., NY. p.285.
    Campbell, I., Lyons, E. and Prescott, R. Stopping Smoking: Do nicotine chewing-gum and postal encouragement add to doctors' advice. *The Practitioner* (1987) 231:114–117.
    Jamrozik, K., Fowler, G., Vessey, M., Wald, N. Placebo controlled trial of nicotine chewing gum in general practice. *British Medical Journal* (1984) 289:794–797.

14 STAYING STOPPED FOR GOOD

'When people will not weed their own minds,
they are apt to be overrun with nettles.'

Horace Walpole

WHEN you stop smoking you can expect to go through a couple of days of physical and mental withdrawal, and after that, assuming that you are dealing with it correctly, your desire to smoke will begin to diminish. First of all, it diminishes in frequency, so you get longer gaps of time in between feeling the desire to smoke. Then, after a week or so, it begins to diminish in intensity as well, so that the sensations you feel will eventually become more like strong thoughts.

Your expectation of how quickly you think your desire should diminish is crucial to your acceptance of it. A few weeks of not smoking can seem like years, and it's helpful to put things into perspective. Expect that your desire might be quite persistent for about as many *days* as the number of *years* you spent smoking. If you look at it that way, the discomfort will seem a lot more reasonable.

Be careful if you make a comparison between smoking and other addictions that you may have conquered. What makes smoking different, and in this regard more difficult, is that it gets so thoroughly integrated into your daily life, and is reinforced frequently over a period of a great many years. That makes the desire to smoke more persistent than almost any other addictive desire.

When you stop smoking, think of the desire to smoke that you experience as being *the result of the sum total of all the cigarettes you ever smoked.*

The more you have smoked, the more persistent your desire to smoke will be. That's why, if you go on smoking, it will never get any easier for you to stop, and why it's best to get out of it as soon as you have the chance to do so.

The Fading Desire

For the first couple of days, while the desire is fairly constant, you will need to find an acceptable compromise between dealing with your desire to smoke and sometimes wanting to have your mind on something else. As the desire begins to lessen, you still need to use the Outline as soon as possible, whenever you notice that your desire has reappeared.

After a few weeks, you may only feel the desire to smoke a few times in a day and it may only last a few minutes, but it's still important to deal with it when it appears; otherwise you will eventually fall back into your old addictive thinking.

One question that is often asked at this stage is: 'How do I know if the desire is really diminishing, or if I'm repressing it?' The answer is found by becoming aware of your attitude towards it.

You can be confident that you're not repressing your desire if you are sincerely welcoming your experience of it. This means opening yourself up to it and letting yourself feel it. It may not be very strong and it may not last for very long, but if you are sincerely willing to feel it, it's not being repressed.

During the first few weeks of not smoking, you can expect to deal with some particularly strong desires because you will encounter a series of 'firsts'. A 'first' is the first time that you are in a particular situation where you used to smoke. There is an immediate connection which produces an intense desire.

When you have only just stopped smoking, the 'firsts' happen in rapid succession: the first time you finish a meal, the first time you get home from work, the first time you answer the phone, the first time you sit and watch TV. Later, the 'firsts' happen less often, but can be surprisingly powerful: the first time you get very angry or disappointed, the first time you visit a particular friend who smokes, or a certain place where you used to smoke.

As the desire fades, you will find that the more persistent desire is associated with certain sorts of situations. For some, their strongest desire to smoke is always first thing in the morning; for others it's late at night. For some, the strongest desire to smoke happens when they are relaxing or out in the evening with friends; for others it's when they are working.

After a while, most of the associations will have faded, and your desire to smoke will rarely, if ever, appear in that particular situation. You may even find yourself reflecting on a recent crisis, and be surprised by the fact that you *didn't* think of smoking at the time.

The situation in which I most often have a desire to smoke is when I am with good friends who smoke. After ten years of not smoking, it has faded so much that the last time I felt a desire to smoke is now quite a few months ago, at a dinner party. It did seem to me, at the time, that smoking a cigarette would be extremely enjoyable.

My desire to smoke lasted about thirty seconds, and I welcomed the mildly uncomfortable sensation, reminding myself that I prefer the better health and greater energy that I have gained as a result of stopping smoking, and that I really like being free from the compulsive, driven quality that characterises addiction to this drug.

I know that I am not immune to the addiction, and I can return to smoking any time. And I am very sure that it's not worth risking the quality of my life for even one puff!

Smokers Smoking

When you see other people smoking, expect to have a desire to smoke yourself. Being in the company of smokers produces some of the most persistent associations. Be very careful of this desire, because when you notice someone else smoking, you will also recall some of your favourite delusions about smoking: 'They only smoke a few cigarettes', 'they do it because it's enjoyable', and — 'it's innocent fun.' If you feel envious of smokers, remind yourself that you have the option of going back to smoking yourself, but remember also the truth behind the delusion. First, although smokers only smoke one cigarette at a time, that cigarette is one of possibly hundreds that they go through every week. *Your desire to smoke is seen as a desire for one cigarette, but in reality it is a desire for one of thousands.*

Smokers may look as though they are enjoying their cigarettes, although the chances are that they are not. Either way, they are compelled to keep smoking them, because otherwise they would have an unsatisfied desire to smoke, which they have not taught themselves to accept.

Not only that, but smokers are in fact perpetually at the beginning of withdrawal, every time a cigarette is extinguished. And what is not immediately apparent is the guilt and fear about smoking that they live with, their deteriorating state of health, their constant broken promises to stop and the loss of self-esteem.

It's essential that you see your desire to smoke for what it is: the automatic, habitual memory of your addiction. Do not confuse it with wanting to return to a life of smoking.

Over to You

If by now you have read the whole of this book, but you have not yet stopped smoking, you may be thinking 'Is this all there is to it?'

A number of clients have told me that, while attending my course, they found themselves with a sense of wanting something more. They also told me that they realised at the time what they were wanting was *to have stopping smoking done for them*. What they really wanted was to be told to stop or somehow made to stop smoking. When they realised that, they also realised that the first decision to begin the process of stopping smoking was, finally, up to them. And when that thought clicked into place, they did choose to stop smoking, and began the process of learning how to stay stopped for good.

If you have now stopped smoking, I suggest you keep reviewing this book, say once a week to begin with, and at least once a month for the first year of your life as an ex-smoker.

Stopping smoking is not a single event: it is a process of re-training your addicted mind. This takes time, and it takes effort, but it is entirely possible for you to succeed completely. The longer you stay stopped, and the more deeply you involve yourself with the techniques in this book, the more likely you are to succeed.

You cannot undo the past. But you can take control of the present. And so determine your future.

In other words   *JIMMY*

I smoked upwards of forty a day for twenty-five years, from the ages of fifteen to forty. Several people said: 'Jimmy will never stop smoking', in those words, while I was a smoker.

I did not want to stop, but thought I had to. I convinced myself that I was a 'natural smoker', but increasingly feared illness.

I had tried acupuncture, hypnosis and willpower alone, with temporary success. I chewed nicotine chewing gum for a year. I stopped, had a jaw like a wrestler, but started smoking again days after stopping chewing.

Full Stop worked, and more than three years later I am still an ex-smoker. I still feel liberated and it's wonderful.

Of course, I still feel the desire to smoke, and I still welcome it. Since doing the course, my life has had its share of problems. One thought that I find vital at moments of crisis is that, if I smoke, I'll just have another problem on my hands.

Acknowledgements

I would like to acknowledge two main sources for the material in this book. One is Joe Zeitchick, who taught me how to stop smoking. The other is the work of Dr K. Bradford Brown and W. Roy Whitten, which helped me broaden my understanding of the processes involved.

Peter Holmes, Peggy Holmes and Patricia Allison have worked with similar techniques and I am grateful to them for their input over the years.

Many thanks go to everyone who helped in various ways with the writing of this book, especially: Gillian Barnett, Dr Roy Eskapa and David Templer. Thanks also to my clients who contributed their own stories about stopping smoking.

Further Help

If you would like information on the Full Stop course or want to give me your experiences of using this book, you can write to me at the following address.

A large (A4) stamped, self-addressed envelope will guarantee you a reply.

Full Stop
PO Box 2484
London
N6 5UX

INDEX